I've admired Caitlin's generosity and her work with The Giving Keys for years. I'm grateful to know her story. It's a reminder to never allow fear or setbacks to keep us from stepping out into the unknown. Caitlin has shown us that it's often in quiet moments of courage that we discover the things we're passionate about and realize more of who we're meant to be.

JOANNA GAINES, cofounder of Magnolia

Caitlin is a force of good in a world that has never needed more people to be real, love their flaws, and unlock their purpose. Her realness has made an impact on me, and I know her incredible story will inspire you to stop letting "perfect" hold you back!

SADIE ROBERTSON, *New York Times* bestselling author, speaker, and founder of Live Original

Smart, funny, relatable, and a master class in finding the courage you need to do the meaningful work you were born for.

BOB GOFF, *New York Times* bestselling author of *Love Does* and *Everybody, Always*

Equal parts powerful and personable, *You Are the Key* tells the story of what is possible when you follow big dreams with big heart.

MARIA SHRIVER, journalist and *New York Times* bestselling author

Caitlin's work in bringing purpose back to the lives of so many speaks for itself. With her as your guide, you will unlock purpose, confidence, and joy beyond what you could ever imagine.

SARAH JAKES ROBERTS, pastor, bestselling author, and founder of Woman Evolve

In this town of glitter, no one's heart and soul shines brighter than Caitlin's. She's given countless men and women their dignity, a sense of purpose, and a second chance at life. She deserves a star on Hollywood Boulevard.

RENE RUSSO, actress, producer, and model

When it comes to changing the world, the notion seems impossible at best—leave it to big business or our political leaders. Caitlin Crosby's *You Are the Key* reminds us that nothing is too far out of reach if we believe in ourselves.

LISA LING, journalist

YOU ARE
the Key

YOU ARE
the Key

TURNING IMPERFECTIONS
INTO PURPOSE

Caitlin Crosby

ZONDERVAN
BOOKS

ZONDERVAN BOOKS

You Are the Key
Copyright © 2020 by Caitlin Crosby Benward

Requests for information should be addressed to:
Zondervan, *3900 Sparks Dr. SE, Grand Rapids, Michigan 49546*

Zondervan titles may be purchased in bulk for educational, business, fundraising, or sales promotional use. For information, please email SpecialMarkets@Zondervan.com.

ISBN 978-0-310-35799-5 (audio)

Library of Congress Cataloging-in-Publication Data

Names: Crosby, Caitlin, author.
Title: You are the key : turning imperfections into purpose / Caitlin Crosby.
Description: Grand Rapids, Michigan : Zondervan, [2020] | Summary: "What if the
    very imperfections you resist the most offer the key to your brightest purpose?
    Join The Giving Keys founder and CEO Caitlin Crosby in You Are the Key
    to discover what happens when we stop hiding our flaws and choose brave
    vulnerability instead"-- Provided by publisher.
Identifiers: LCCN 2020000388 (print) | LCCN 2020000389 (ebook) | ISBN
    9780310357971 (hardcover) | ISBN 9780310357988 (ebook)
Subjects: LCSH: Self-actualization (Psychology) | Vulnerability (Personality trait) |
    Self-acceptance.
Classification: LCC BF637.S4 C757 2020 (print) | LCC BF637.S4 (ebook) | DDC
    158.1--dc23
LC record available at https://lccn.loc.gov/2020000388
LC ebook record available at https://lccn.loc.gov/2020000389

Author is represented by Cait Hoyt at CAA.

Cover design: Curt Diepenhorst
Cover photo: Trever Hoehne
Interior design: Kait Lamphere

Printed in the United States of America

20 21 22 23 24 25 26 27 28 29 30 /LSC/ 15 14 13 12 11 10 9 8 7 6 5 4 3 2 1

Dedicated to my momma,
Patricia Townsend Crosby.

Thank you for taking me to all the LA homeless
shelters in my youth to teach me the importance
of giving, and for reading me The Giving Tree
thousands of times. Your empathy, sensitivity,
and heart made me who I am.

CONTENTS

Introduction: How to Be a Person 11

1. No MBA Needed 19
2. Playing Undercover 43
3. Listen to Your Peace-o-Meter 57
4. A Man's World 75
5. The Surprise of Surrender 89
6. Make Yourself Proud 111
7. Girl Boss in the ER 129
8. Save Your Savior Complex 153
9. Scarred & Hard 169
10. Imperfect Is the New Perfect 189
11. Let Yourself Fail 201
12. Can't Burn Down Love 213

HOW TO BE A PERSON

Your vocation in life is where your greatest
joy meets the world's greatest need.
—Frederick Buechner

ook, sometimes being a human can be difficult. Can I get
an amen?

Does anyone else feel like it is challenging enough to simply
prioritize the everyday responsibilities of being alive, much less figure out the point of our existence? Like fighting through the over-
whelm, exhaustion, and messiness of life to muster up the strength
to take care of your mind, body, soul; or run the necessary updates
on your computer (yes, "remind me tomorrow")?

To complicate this even further, most of us want more from
life than going through the motions. More than checking the box
of becoming "successful," we want *meaning*. We want to know that
our days *matter*, and that they are building something beautiful.

For as long as I can remember, I wanted to do something that
mattered in the world. I wanted to take my adversity, challenges,
and pain and make a difference in people's lives. To work on

something bigger than myself. As cliché as it sounds, I was determined to make the world a better place.

The problem is, the older I get, the more I realize how truly challenging it is to "change the world" when you're busy figuring out how to simply make it through the day. When you're still figuring out how to be a *human*. Baby steps, right?

From the outside looking in, you might think of me as having my life all together. Maybe you know of my giveback social enterprise called The Giving Keys or have heard my music, seen me on a TV a time or two, or seen a filtered photo of me on Instagram. What you may not know is what life has been like for me beneath the surface, which is probably not all that different from what life is like for you on a day-to-day basis. I look at myself in the mirror, disgusted with secret deformities of my body; I fight with my husband; and, yes, my baby's poop sometimes gets smeared all over our walls, and I may or may not leave it there until the unforeseeable future, when I can catch my breath.

I know I'm not alone in this. I meet men and women all the time who tell me they dream of making the world a better place. They might tell me that they're passionate and full of ambition to go after their idea or make a big change, but that they don't have the know-how, time, money, or experience to live the full life they desire. Sometimes they even whisper to me about some shame they're carrying, something they think will keep them from ever making their contribution to the world. They tell me they admire what I've done with The Giving Keys and hope they, too, can "change the world." Meanwhile, I wonder if they know exactly what they're saying.

Hi, I'm Caitlin. Founder and CEO of The Giving Keys, former actress, singer-songwriter, wife to Colin, and mother to Brave and Love—who also struggles, just like you may, with existential crises, severe insecurity, hairy legs (and toes), meltdowns, feeling like a failure, and days where everything feels like the weight of the world is on my shoulders and I'm about to crash and burn (and have a literal heart attack).

Whew. I said that all in one breath.

No matter who you are or what you're facing, I believe deep in my soul that every person is here for a reason. I've also come to believe, as I've gotten older and life has gotten harder, that it can be difficult to keep that passion for purpose ignited. We accumulate scars that run deep—sometimes too deep for any ultra-strength cocoa butter to rub away (I mean that both figuratively and literally). In the midst of the daily stressors of raising a family, running a business, and being betrayed by people I trust, I find it difficult at times to keep my hope and inspiration alive. I imagine you do, too. Sometimes I worry that my life is passing me by and that maybe, just maybe, I was wrong all along.

But amidst all of the challenges, I can't shake the notion that my life has a destination, a purpose—and that yours does, too. It's hard to see through the fog sometimes, but I believe it's worth fighting through to live the life we were meant to.

In this book, we will explore what "purpose" even means. How will you measure your life? Is it only the macro, mountain-top experiences, or can it be found in the simplicity of being content with what you already have? How would trusting your own unique purpose change the way you live? How would it change the way you see yourself? I know it might seem completely improbable to you. It certainly has to me. But not anymore. Not after everything I'm about to tell you.

This book is my way of saying to you, *You have a purpose, and it's waiting for you. It's not too late. There's more out there for you. You do have what it takes. Your life is here, in the now, and it's waiting for you.*

I know this because, like you, I've questioned my own purpose, resisted it, missed it completely, and then found it buried in the most unlikely place. There *is* a reason you're here on this earth. There's something you, and only you, can contribute to our little planet. Finding it requires a journey of sorts. A journey within your own heart and soul. When you look—really *look*—at your possibly messy and beautifully broken story, you will find what you've been looking for. *You will be able to turn your trials into your testimony.*

Here's the biggest catch of all. Most people go looking for purpose in their highlight reels, childhood dreams, and proudest moments. I'm not saying you can't find some evidence of your purpose there. But what I'll demonstrate in this book is how often we find our purpose in the exact *opposite* place. The place we're least likely to look.

Usually it's found in those less-than-flattering moments—the dark times, the wanderings, the failures, the emptiness, the searching, the times you came completely to the end of your rope and didn't know what to do next. It's found in the thing you did that you swore you would never tell anyone. In the thing done *to you* that you swore you would never tell anyone. You look away, pretend it never happened, put on a smile and act (as we all sometimes do) like everything is "fine." But under the surface, there's something nagging at your soul. Something shameful, something embarrassing, something vulnerable. There's beauty and freedom there. Look there.

Often, our purpose and our "life's work" meets us in those dark places. The question is, are we willing to dig deep and take the journey?

Sure, I've had a few accomplishments that I'm proud of. I'm sure you have, too. But it's the wild, messy ones that have shaped me the most.

I'll save the deep, heart-wrenching stories for later, but for starters, how about the time I accidentally voice memo texted a huge fight with my husband to my entire leadership team? Another time, I got pink-eye from my son and gave it to all of my employees. Or how about the terrifying day when a disgruntled employee brought a gun into our office—a gun he intended to use on us? No one prepares you to navigate a life-or-death situation like that. Talk about feeling vulnerable and underqualified. No one was hurt that day, but the oversight on my part—and the guilt I've carried since—is just one of so many failures. They often seem to pile up.

Dare I mention the occasion I sucked my son's baby food purée out of a plastic pouch just to make it through the day since I hadn't prioritized eating like a normal adult? Maybe that one was actually genius. My entrepreneur mind automatically started thinking about how to create a line of food pouches that would be socially acceptable to consume for "adult humans on the go."

On top of all this, for all of my life I've had a secret "flaw" I've been hiding. I'm going to share it with you in this book. I've never talked about it before, but I've decided it's time, if only because this flaw is (as yours is) the key to my hidden beauty and strength.

Still, there are bad days. Even as I write this book—a message I believe in with every fiber of my being—I've been swimming through murky waters and trying to keep my head above water as a wife, mom, and business owner. Having overcome so many hurdles has brought me a peace that passes understanding. But I won't try to tell you it's been easy.

Your journey of discovering and developing your purpose won't be a straight line or math equation. It doesn't usually work like that. It's all curvy lines, highs and lows, and there are parts where you can't even tell up from down. There are very few moments in life, if any, when we feel calmly and plainly that we've fully arrived.

You'll get some bumps and bruises. You'll experience some painful failures. You'll question yourself. You'll fall down, and with resilience you will get back up again. That's the key to all of this. You can't give up on yourself when you're in the dark place. It's in the "dark place" where your purpose is found.

I hope I can teach you how to see differently in the dark, the way I learned to see differently in the dark.

You might feel discouraged, worthless, or insecure about your brain, body, work, the life you're building. But if you're reading this book, I already know you have it in you to stand up, dust yourself off, and start each day anew. You have what it takes to create a life that's meaningful and inspire others to do the same.

There are two things I really want you to know as we begin this journey together.

First, I want you to know that you don't have to be perfect to have a purpose. Quite the opposite, in fact. Your imperfections are talking to you. Your imperfections *are* your key. They can unlock all the joy, creativity, beauty, depth, vulnerability, and life you've been waiting for.

And here's the real kicker: the world *needs* your imperfect. What it *doesn't* need is more of the picture-perfect.

Second, I want you to know that your career is not the same as your purpose. It may be part of it for a season of time. And sure, it may align or overlap. But we must be careful to not get too attached to a career or movement we've created, because those things change. We don't want our identity to get wrapped up in what we do, because that can be a slippery slope. I can tell you right now, The Giving Keys is not my purpose. The Giving Keys is *part* of my purpose. It could crash and burn tomorrow, or I could decide to close it down to focus on my family, because The Giving Keys doesn't define me as a human being. Our purpose goes deeper than our day job. It's about what brings us alive as we bring life to the world.

My hope for you is that this book will be a companion to you on your journey, a catalyst for asking the questions, a conversation-starter, an excuse to laugh, and a support to you as you seek your own answers. Because the world needs you—the abilities, talents and gifts you have. The world needs your imperfection. Think of it this way: You are God's work of art, here for a unique reason to live out a calling that only you can. Imagine your purpose out there in the world like a tiny hidden treasure, locked in a box. *You* are the key to the treasure.

And now, it's time to unlock the treasure.

chapter one

NO MBA NEEDED

Do not wait for leaders; do it
alone, person to person.
—Mother Teresa

I meet people all the time who want to start something. Maybe
it's a "Time's Up" or "Me Too" movement. Maybe it's a political campaign. Maybe it's about racism, bullying, eating disorders,
or fertility issues. Maybe it's about gun laws. Maybe it's a non-
judgmental, inclusive church where people are celebrated in all of
their humanity, struggles, and strengths. Maybe a nonprofit. Maybe
it's an Etsy shop selling knitted baby hats, or a blog, or a group of
women gathering regularly to share dinner and stories. Whatever it
is, I also hear a thousand perfectly beautiful ideas from people like
you every year and just as many justifications for why those ideas
would never work:

"I don't have any money . . ."
"I don't have any experience . . ."

"I don't have the background . . ."
"I'm busy with a full-time job . . ."
"I'm busy being a full-time mom . . ."

What they don't realize is that anyone who has ever started anything is starting exactly where they're starting—right where they are.

I don't mean to make light of the fact that some people have access to more resources than others. Some have access to certain people or information, and some have more education and training to help get them moving in the right direction. All *four* of my best friends have MBAs, for example, and sometimes I find myself thinking. "wouldn't *that* be nice—to have some actual training for running a business!" All of that education and wisdom could have really come in handy as we started to scale The Giving Keys. Then I remind myself: That was their path, and this is mine. There is more than one right way to do something. Who knows, I may go back to school later in life.

There's nothing wrong with getting an MBA, obviously. Or any other kind of degree. It's incredible to be given the opportunity to further your education, and it can only help you to gain as much training and wisdom as possible—something others may not have access to. I think some people are meant to continue their education in order to be able to fill the role they're meant to play in both the world and their vocation. I also believe we far too often get stuck in the trap of *thinking* we need a particular kind of training on something to get started when what we really need is the bravery to actually *get started*. An MBA is great. But an MBA doesn't do you much good if you never actually have the courage to take action.

So MBA or no MBA, I wanted to share my story with you to demonstrate that if you don't have the means to get an MBA, or the opportunity, or the time, or if you simply don't want to, that's OK. You still have everything you need inside to make the world a better place like only *you* can.

I can't say there's a perfect formula. But I can tell you I've spent the last two (or more) decades of my life "trying again"—even at times when all evidence seemed to point to the fact that I should quit. I've started passion projects that turned into businesses, with and without the exact resources most of us are worried about: Time. Money. Experience. Background.

There are a handful of things people will say you need in order to start something, and the one I hear most often is a "business plan." These people are usually adamant that you need to know revenue models or have cash flow spreadsheets and act like it's not worth even trying if you don't have a respectable stamp of approval from Harvard. But the truth is, I started a business with *none* of that and founded a multi-million-dollar internationally recognized giveback brand that has helped over 130 people transition out of homelessness and over a million people find hope through the pay it forward model.

I don't say any of this to point out how smart or great I am. I say it to point out how smart and magical *you* are—how much more capable you are than you give yourself credit for. I believe most of the excuses running through your mind for why you're feeling like you haven't found your peace or place in the world and could never start the thing you want to start are all lies. They will keep your business (and your healing, your dreams, your freedom, your peace, your purpose) stuck.

In fact, if there is one common denominator I've identified in all of my friends or colleagues who are making their way in the world, changing industries, and shaking up culture, it's this: They've all seen problems and obstacles as opportunities. They've *all* taken a chance on something they were passionate about when it didn't make perfect sense.

One of my friends, Allison Trowbridge, with whom I host the podcast *Real Good Company* and who got her MBA from Oxford (which was very Harry Potter of her), calls it a "divine scavenger hunt"—always following those heart taps and going through those open doors that you intuitively know are meant for you. The special ideas, the ones that really make waves, are always out-of-the-box. The people who have those ideas have also gotten it wrong; have had to pivot; have fallen, gotten up, and tried again.

MBA or no MBA, don't let what you don't have hold you back from your calling.

My favorite book growing up was *The Giving Tree* by Shel Silverstein. My mother tells me I used to ask her to read it over and over again. She makes sure I remember that even as a little girl, the book made me cry. (Have you ever met a CEO of a multi-million-dollar company who frequently bursts into tears in the middle of staff meetings? Now you have.) According to Mom, I'd sit there on the couch, snuggled up into the crook of her arm, tears streaming down my face while she flipped the pages. I couldn't get enough of the tree's bleeding heart to serve the boy until he had nothing left. Then, as soon as she read the last word, I'd scream, "Again! Again!" I guess some things never change.

If you've read the book, you know what it's about. But in case you haven't, or in case it's been awhile, it's a beautiful depiction of a little boy and his special tree, the giving tree.

The tree is happy when it can make the boy happy. When he's a young boy, it provides him with a shady playground and apples to eat. When the boy grows to be a man, he's unsatisfied with his life and demands the tree's wood in order to make a boat, which the tree happily provides, allowing itself to be cut down. Eventually, the man finds himself coming back to the tree's stump to rest and find peace. Even at a young age, I knew what this meant—that satisfaction can never be found in the things we try to take from this world but rather in what we have to give to it. This is a powerful lesson for all of us. Have you considered the answer to the question, what do you have to *give* the world?

The book shows the sacrificial love of the giving tree through each stage of the boy's life, and honestly, it still moves me today. Somehow, despite my deep love for the book, I went thirty years without reading it. Then, almost everyone I knew bought me the book for my baby shower, so I now read it to my little boy, Brave, to continue the tradition. Life sometimes gets away from us, but then it tends to come back around, doesn't it? Just when you think you've lost your way, life shows you the path.

Now, when I read to my son, I'm reminded of why I loved *The Giving Tree* so much and of the profound impact it's had on my life. Although now I also ponder whether the tree would have been a bit better off with a little more self-care, boundaries, and balance. I love the picture the book paints of what it looks like to be all in, full-hearted, and ready to serve. Sometimes giving is rewarding, and other times, it takes sacrifice (and sometimes, if the pendulum swings too far, you may "over-give," which can be detrimental to your health. Hello, me). The message of this book seeped into my soul as a little girl and still drives what I do today at The Giving Keys.

So when I think about a business plan (or just a life plan) and how much it matters if you want to start something, I'm not denying a plan could be helpful. I am saying that you can easily create a makeshift business plan from a template you pull from the internet in a single afternoon using a Sharpie on a napkin. What you *can't* pull from the internet is character, and the authentic empathy necessary for the passion and commitment it takes to answer the call on your life. What you can't pull from the internet is a heart of service, the fire of purpose that keeps you going even when it seems like the world is spinning fast and you're running on no sleep and you can barely get half a shower in the morning without someone desperately needing something from you (I'm looking at you, moms). You can't find *that* on a Google spreadsheet.

Giving has been a pillar, a focus in my life as I've found my way and my career. This right-brained philosophy major who didn't finish college was not *supposed* to become a CEO—but I did. And like it or not, the crying thing has stayed with me, too. I even feel proud of it because, over time, I've realized my tears, passion, and raw emotions are my great strength, not my weakness. I would not have been able to create the things I have without this sensitive heart of mine.

Could your number one weakness be your greatest strength as well?

What I'd like you to do is ditch everything you think you know about what it takes to run a business or pursue a dream or vocation. If you ever feel you don't have what it takes, welcome to the club. If you worry you don't have enough experience, skills, connections, money, or time to pursue a career or idea stirring in you, I'm here to tell you that you have *everything you need* right now to start.

I grew up in Los Angeles—actually, all over the LA area—as my parents separated from each other three or four-ish times. I lived everywhere from Brentwood, to my grandparents' house in Woodland Hills, to West Hollywood, then back to Woodland Hills, to Malibu visiting my dad on weekends, to seedy Hollywood (where drug deals and shootings were happening in our driveway), and everywhere in between.

When I was sixteen, my parents got back together, so we moved again, this time to an apartment in Beverly Hills—9021(1). So close.

I lived in some nice areas, but my family dynamics were pretty tumultuous, which was confusing for me as a child. We'd move houses, and I'd start at a new school, trying to make new friends all over again (so, yes, I would sometimes eat lunch with teachers or just stand in the vending machine line or lunch line over and over again so I wouldn't have to sit down by myself).

My parents worked hard to get me into safer school districts. And by "safer," I mean schools that didn't have metal detectors at every entrance.

When my mom and dad met, my mom was a model and an actress, and my dad was a talent agent. My dad helped discover everyone from George Clooney, to Rene Russo, to Charlize Theron, to Shia LaBeouf. He represented The Rolling Stones' lead singer, Mick Jagger, as well as Jim Morrison, when they were both testing the acting waters. Needless to say, I had some pretty big shoes to fill. I can remember thinking to myself, "If only I could be as beautiful and talented as Charlize," I would be worthy of my father's time and love. In my early teen years, I wanted badly to be an actress because I thought that's what value, success, and worth looked like.

As a teenager, I nervously covered my acne with caked-on makeup, wore hats, and arranged my hair so that it covered my face to go to castings and my father's client's film premieres. I constantly felt like I was in the shadows of his clients. I felt I had to meet a certain standard of perfection. After all, he had so many successful clients—how could I, his own daughter, not measure up?

I needed to be Charlize-Theron-good and Charlize-Theron-beautiful and Charlize-Theron-talented. All that time, while I was trying to live up to Charlize, I never once considered that I could have a totally different purpose. That perhaps my own purpose would be altogether missed as long as I was trying so desperately to be like Charlize. But at the time, I didn't even let myself consider those questions.

Still, in the midst of my expectations of greatness, I also saw many things that happened behind the scenes that I didn't want. Things like my dad bailing out his clients from jail in the middle of the night and working hard to keep it out of the press. I saw how fame and money didn't buy happiness for people. I also saw dozens of actresses struggling with body image—and realized I wasn't alone in that battle. Sadly, there was this constant comparison of ourselves to the so-called "perfect," ideal, sexy, airbrushed women on magazines and billboards.

All this to say, I may have grown up around fame and fortune, but the celebrity influence wounded me more than it helped. I never felt like I was enough.

One slap-in-the-face moment made me realize I wanted to do something about the body image issues I experienced and saw so many other women dealing with. I landed my first leading role in a feature film with Danny DeVito alongside Brie Larson. When the movie poster came out, Brie and I saw that our faces had been cut out and pasted on other women's bodies. We never even wore the outfits on the movie poster bodies. They just slapped our faces on airbrushed, idealistic women's bodies.

For me, this was the breaking point. In my mind, enough was enough. I knew someone needed to do something—and why shouldn't it be me? So Brie and I decided to start a movement called Love Your Flawz (LoveYourFlawz.com) to bring a different stance on body image to the world. The idea behind Love Your Flawz was to create a space and opportunity for women to celebrate their flaws instead of comparing themselves to the unfair standards of beauty set by the media and others. It was a chance for people to share their so-called "imperfections" and to change their perspectives and narratives into a positive view of their uniquenesses. (I now wouldn't even call them flaws.)

I also started early in the music business as a singer-songwriter and professional awkward dancer. Years later, when I honed my guitar skills, I was on music tour as a solo artist and started taking pictures of people who came to the shows, helping them make signs to hold up, sayings things like:

"My acne is beautiful."
"My chemo-fried hair is a sign of my strength."
"My scar saved my life."
"My cellulite is sexy."
"My cankles are the new black."
"Learning to love my love handles."
"I'm not a size 0 or size 2 or even a 4 or a 6. And that's OK."

And by "signs," I mean I'd find scraps, like used receipts from the bar or toilet paper, and ask around for a pen so people could make their new mantras. It started to spread, and all kinds of people started taking their own pictures from home and submitting them to the site. It was a small step to take, but it has had ripple effects of positivity for thousands of people.

The truth is, you don't need an MBA to jumpstart your passion. We all start somewhere, and we all have scars from our past. But you don't need to take an extravagant step toward your idea, or any practice in your life. You just need to start small. Start with what you already have, with what naturally lights up your heart. Or start with something you're fighting for in your own personal life—something you think others might be fighting for as well. The point is, don't wait until you feel flawless to get started. Your flaws are your window, your hint, your great gift, and your key to the bright future ahead.

My whole life, I've prayed, *God, I want to feel what you feel for people. Break my heart so I feel for people exactly what you feel for them.* Little did I know where that would lead me. Love Your Flawz was only the beginning.

A few years later, I was touring around the country for my music album. One week, I stayed in a New York motel, and the key to my room was huge, old, and rusted. At one point, I thought I had lost the key, so I asked the front desk for a new one. Then, when I got to the next state, I found the original key in my bag. Because I loved the uniqueness of the key and the memories attached to it, I decided to add it to my necklace chain, and slipped it over my neck. The rush of compliments that key received completely surprised me. After all, it was just a key. Or so I thought.

Back home in Los Angeles, I was at a locksmith one day, and I heard the person in front of me ask to get his apartment number engraved on his key. I asked the locksmith if he had letters, and if he could engrave LOVE YOUR FLAWZ on that old, rusted key. (That was clearly my thing at the time.) The key was already special, but now the necklace became one-of-a-kind.

While at the locksmith, I noticed a pile of other old, used keys that were discarded off to the side, seemingly with no use anymore. I casually asked if he could engrave them with other words like HOPE, STRENGTH, COURAGE, FIGHT, BELIEVE, FEARLESS, PEACE, DREAM, and FAITH.

I was planning to give them to friends as inspirational gifts.

He charged me eight dollars total per key—three dollars for each blank key and five to do the engraving. I then went to my local bead shop and bought some chain rolls, suede cords, leather scraps, clasps, and wires to attach the clasps. With the help of my personal cuticle clippers and tweezers (that's called budgeting and makin' it work, people), I began making jewelry to give to my friends and family.

Then, I started getting compliments and countless requests for more of these engraved key necklaces.

The most special things we create are always born out of love.

When it was time for my next music tour, I decided to sell an assortment of the engraved key jewelry at the merchandise tables, alongside my CDs. From the stage, between songs, I talked to the audience about embracing our imperfections. The more I talked about it, the more I began to realize that we are all like keys: unique, flawed, scarred, and at risk of being discarded. I asked listeners to find and wear a key that would remind them that they were also one-of-a-kind.

Every night, from state to state, the key necklaces started selling out faster than my CDs. (I tried not to be offended!) Suddenly, before every show, instead of rehearsing and tuning my guitar, I found myself scrambling to find more keys and assemble chains and clasps with my cuticle clippers and tweezers, just to keep up with the demand. It was fascinating to me and intriguing how much people needed the symbolic message behind the keys.

Part of me was wondering, *What on earth am I doing?!* The other part of me *knew* I was onto something that was resonating with people. Then, I had a *new* idea for the key necklaces.

I started encouraging people to give their necklace to someone they felt needed the message on that particular key more than themselves. So basically, you would wear a key that said STRENGTH until you met someone who needed that message more than you, and then you'd pass the key on to that person, paying it forward. Now the keys were becoming stories. They were unlocking opportunities for conversations. They were developing a whole life of their own.

I realized that with every key passed to someone else, there was a story. People started writing me messages on MySpace (yes, MySpace, which proves we are the OG's) sharing their heart-wrenching stories of how and why they had given their keys away. Beautiful, descriptive, inspiring messages began to pour in by the day.

A story about someone who was battling thoughts of suicide when a friend gave her a key that said HOPE. A story of a woman whose daughter was in the hospital, sick and unsure if she would make it. Her friend took the key off her own neck and placed it around the mom's neck. It said COURAGE. These and other stories showed the power behind a simple act of looking at the people around you—really paying attention to what they're experiencing—and of being willing to give someone a token of encouragement and care: HOPE, LOVE, DREAM, FIGHT, BELIEVE.

I kept thinking how powerful it would be if people had a public place to share their key stories so other people could read them, connect, and be touched. By "people," I mean people other than my mom and me. So I created TheGivingKeys.com, a place where people could post the stories of their keys being passed around the world.

It was incredible. It was profoundly special. It was magic. I was hooked.

Still, I knew there was a missing link. The impact of The Giving Keys was obvious, but I wanted to find more ways to make it even more original.

This is an important part of the story, because I could have easily settled for what The Giving Keys was in those early days. It was already so unique and powerful—I could have just let it be and continued to run with the pay it forward mission. But I kept feeling in my gut that there was something else to it. I trusted that feeling, and I'm so glad I did.

Whatever you're pursuing in your life, I encourage you to not settle. Push the envelope even further. How can you make it a little bit more unique and interesting? How can you add that differentiating factor? And if you're wondering where on earth an idea like this is going to come from, I won't make you wonder much longer: it's going to come from deep inside you. From your failures, your story, your quirks, your sensitivities, your "flaws," the things about you that you're perhaps most *un*likely to share.

You are the key.

The revenue from the keys was originally going into the "merch sales" envelope, and being sent back to my record label, but when I started selling them at other events, I decided the money from the sales should go to a charity or some special cause. But how would I decide *what* charity or cause, and what would that actually look like? I had quite a few friends who had started nonprofits, and I could easily have made the model something like, "We donate 10 percent of every sale to . . . XYZ company," but I just kept sensing that wasn't quite right. I even felt like that was settling.

Not long after making that decision, I attended a screening of the documentary *Invisible Children*, about child soldiers in Uganda, at Ecclesia Church on Hollywood Boulevard. After it was over, I walked out into the rain and headed to my car. My face was red and puffy from crying. Yes, tears again. You're not surprised. But after watching that film, I felt like I was on fire. I wanted to change the world. I wanted to help. Right there, right then. I was bursting with passion for humanity.

Right there on Hollywood Boulevard, I prayed the prayer, *God, what else can I do to help people?*

That's when I saw them. There was a couple, soaking wet, holding up a sign which caught my eye, mostly because it reminded me of the Love Your Flawz signs all those beautiful souls made while I was out on tour. This one said "Ugly, Broke, and Hungry." Feeling compelled by something beyond me, I walked over to the couple and introduced myself. And as soon as I met them, I fell in love. They were the key, the missing link of The Giving Keys.

Their names are Cera and Rob. They were twenty-three at the time, and as they started to tell me their stories, I was so compelled I had to hear more. I cancelled my plans for the evening and asked if I could take them to dinner at a swanky restaurant nearby.

I know what you're thinking. *Wait, you did* what *with two homeless strangers?* But the truth is, this wasn't at all abnormal for me. In fact, because of the homelessness epidemic in LA, from the time I was young, I was passionate about simply hearing the stories of people who were living on the streets. Maybe it had to do with all the moving around I did as a kid, maybe it was all the missions my mom took me to as a child, maybe it was the church youth group I was raised in, maybe it was that idea of *The Giving Tree*, or that prayer, but seeing the hurting people others passed by absolutely broke my heart. I could not ignore it.

If there was some way—any way—I could possibly offer love, encouragement, or even food at the very least, I wanted to do it. My heart seemed to draw me right to them. This is often right where we find our alignment and our purpose, right where we want to be.

Years before I started The Giving Keys, I wrote a song for my first album called "Same Inside" based on a woman I'd met outside a Starbucks who was experiencing homelessness. (FYI, I learned early on in the homelessness advocacy community that it's not appropriate to label anyone as "homeless." It's best to say someone is "experiencing homelessness," so that it's not defining who they are. In general, I've learned that it's better to go beyond labels when you're referring to *anyone*, because labels do not dignify the human spirit. We are all so much more than our circumstances.) Every night on tour, before the song, I would explain to the audience that I had a long conversation with this woman about her life, and afterward, I asked if I could buy her any food, and she said, "No thank you. Thank you for just talking and listening to me." I was so touched, thinking that perhaps we, as humans, are all craving the same thing: to be heard, seen, and loved. Whether you're living on the streets or in a mansion, we are all the same in that way. I went home and wrote:

I bought a new blanket
Though I have three others
We're getting used to this hierarchy
I'm paid to walk a mile
When you run it for free
Turn my cheek, though your hand is open
I've got a busy week so I cling to my tokens

Throw some scraps from under my table
Just one smile would keep you warm
Thought I had you pinned you under a label
Might a conversation end this storm?

With no place to run
And no place to hide
Everyone screaming "Divide"
With no place to go

When you don't have a home
But we're all just the same inside
We're all just the same inside

So when, years later, I saw Cera and Rob, I just *knew*. It was the same thing that drew me to the woman outside Starbucks. Something in me knew I had to keep talking to them. I needed to know more about their stories.

When I took them to dinner that night, I ordered a glass of red wine. Rob and Cera each ordered beers—one called *Hop-Apocalypse* and the other called *Zombie Rager*. We ate salmon and New York strip steak and sat talking together while I watched this couple enjoy the best meal they'd had in ages. It was a beautiful reminder of how I take for granted much of the food I'm lucky enough to eat. It was a reminder to always relish every single bite.

As we got to know each other, I complimented Cera on her necklace. She said she had made it herself. In that instant, a light bulb went off in my mind. I had the biggest *aha* moment right there in the restaurant. I flung my hands in the air and screamed, "You guys are the missing link to The Giving Keys! Do you want to be my business partners?"

I think they were surprised and confused at first, and understandably so. Then I showed them The Giving Keys website, and we were off to the races.

The day after I met Cera and Rob, I went back to the locksmith and begged him to help me order an engraving kit from his vendor connection. I then bought hammers at Pep Boys so Rob and Cera could start engraving. We started meeting at various FedExes, Kinko's, post offices, Carl's Jr. parking lots, unsafe alleyways, and transitional homes to work on the project. I taught them my basic process for making the necklaces (I finally splurged and bought them real jewelry pliers, because you know a girl's gotta keep her tweezers handy at all times) and they started making the products on their own. Once they became pros, and I saw how hard they worked and how trustworthy they were, I started handing over more and more responsibility.

It 100 percent looked like we were doing drug deals every time we met. I'd roll down my window, hand them some cash, they would hand me a small paper bag, and onlookers would give us the most shameful looks. If only they knew what was inside.

We created a pretty reliable process for our workflow, and I even garnered major street cred for learning how to pack like real deal drug dealers do. Each necklace was packed tightly into ripped-up pieces of used plastic bag that was then twisted up and tied in a knot. All stacked on top of each other in one dirty, see-through plastic bag, they looked like a full-blown drug smuggle worth thousands.

Though I thoroughly enjoyed the *Breaking-Bad*-in-real-life lessons, I knew we needed to improve our system.

Meanwhile, Rob and Cera were innovative. They upped their game and started to cut little slits in their microwavable dinner boxes to hang the necklaces in so they wouldn't get tangled. *Brilliant.* The keys kept selling (although some now smelled of chicken pot pie). They also kept getting passed along to others, and Cera and Rob now had full-time jobs.

They started saving their money, and soon they were able to start staying in the Mark Twain Motel in Hollywood. Meanwhile, I started selling the jewelry anywhere people would let me: other musicians' shows, birthday parties, charity events, garage sales, book launches, local flea markets. Then I started getting them into some of the most popular boutiques in the US, with literally *no* retail sales experience.

I was a barista at the trendsetting Fred Segal store, so I *kind of* knew the buyer, Karen, because I made her lattes. (Buyer is the job title of the person who decides what products to carry in a store.) I would casually wear about twenty keys around my wrists and neck and on my ears, hoping she would notice. Finally, one day she said, "Wow, those are fabulous! Who makes those?"

As I dramatically brushed my hair back, I said, "Oh, these? Funny you should ask. I'm trying to get this one couple who is experiencing homelessness off the streets by selling them."

To my complete surprise and delight, she said, "We should sell them here! What's your wholesale price?" I didn't even know what that meant, so I told her whatever she wanted to sell them for is fine with me! And we were off to the races. Don't need no MBA, indeed.

Karen showed me the ropes and introduced me to our first showroom rep. I was as green as green could be, but the truth is, once other stores caught wind that we were in THE Fred Segal, they thought The Giving Keys was a *professional jewelry company.* Now everyone wanted this new, trendy jewelry in their stores. Just like that, we started to take off.

Little by little, as Rob and Cera kept making money and saving it, they both started GED classes. Rob, who was actually born and raised on the streets, ended up scoring in the ninety-ninth percentile and registered to start community college.

I want to stop here for a minute and say that this just goes to show me how much untapped potential is in the people most of us overlook. Imagine what we would have missed if Rob and Cera hadn't been given a chance? Imagine what we might be missing by not giving a fair shot to all the people in our communities who are so easy to overlook? Who will you pass by today who needs a little bit of encouragement, a little support, or a little love in order to unlock their true intelligence and talent? You can be the one who helps them get there.

Still working full-time for The Giving Keys, Rob and Cera saved up enough money to get their first apartment—all because one night I watched a film, my heart hurt for the brokenness I saw all around me, and I decided to follow my instinct to walk over and say hello.

Not to mention—and this is something people *don't* always mention when they talk about "following your passion" or finding your career path or finding a way to use your gifts to give and serve—the truth is that my own heart has been healed and continues to be healed in the process as much as anyone else's. I think that's why my heart was calling me to go talk to Rob and Cera that day. Not just because *they* needed *me*, but because *I* needed *them*. All the people I've worked with over the years at The Giving Keys have given me far more than I've ever given to them. We need each other.

My point is this: I didn't know how to start when I started. I just started. I didn't know the "right" way to do things. I just did them. I didn't know how to employ people. Every smart business person would say (Hiring 101), *Don't hire homeless people*. I knew nothing about the fashion or jewelry industry when this all started. I just started. I paid attention to my motives and my heart. I let my heart break for the people in my city experiencing homelessness and decided to take action. You don't need no MBA.

Not long after I hired Rob and Cera, we couldn't keep up with orders, so I started hiring more people straight off the streets. Yes, my parents were constantly worried, but it was *working*. After a couple of years of trial and error and partnering with churches, we started partnering with well-known, respected nonprofits who focused their work and service around the issue of homelessness.

They started screening candidates for me to interview and

start training. It was helpful to incorporate trained, professional case managers into the process at this point, to help support some of the challenges that would inevitably arise from hiring this demographic (aside from my *very* professional approach, which sometimes involved showing up at their hotel rooms to find alcohol bottles in their beds, and then I'd start crying).

We implemented drug testing and other necessary screenings into our hiring process. All the while, we kept hiring more people to keep up with the orders, and we've now hired more than a hundred and thirty people who are transitioning out (or have already successfully transitioned out) of homelessness. The Giving Keys have been sold at Starbucks, Nordstrom, and Bloomingdale's, as well as over a thousand other stores around the world, and we've now sold close to two million keys.

The goal is to keep expanding The Giving Keys to get as many people employed and off the streets as possible, and for lives to be impacted positively every time a key is passed on to encourage and inspire. I go online every day to read the stories of how people's lives are made better by a simple act of kindness—giving a key— and every one reminds me what life is all about. When a friend or family member gives away their key, their word, to someone who needs it more, it's a hope movement. It's proof that there is good in this world.

My encouragement to you is to keep your eyes open to the needs of those around you. They are all over the place. I love what Mother Teresa said: "Do not wait for leaders; do it alone, person to person." It could be as simple as seeing someone on the street who's hungry and getting them some food. If you see someone who's cold, give them a blanket—I'm sure you have a few extras in your closet. But don't do it because you're trying to come up with an innovative new organization, or because you want to become a social entrepreneur, or you want to start a nonprofit. No, it needs to be based on a true inner desire to care about other people.

When people ask my advice on how to start a nonprofit or passion project, I always say to start first by caring deeply about an issue or injustice you see in the world or in your community. Build the idea around that, not the other way around. Aid the cause.

Consumers can smell when a business or organization is just adding a charitable component to beef up the bottom line or to keep up with the trend of being a "social entrepreneur" or start a "giveback brand." People will smell it if you really don't deeply care about the issue. They'll also smell it when you *do,* and your authentic passion for the mission will compel them to care and to take action with you.

Even if you don't see yourself at the helm of a new start-up or initiative, I believe it's worth it for all of us to discover what your heart breaks for. There are plenty of injustices in the world to get fired up about. Our world is riddled with the struggles associated with poverty, human trafficking, access to clean water, bullying, education, gun violence, drug addiction, climate change, politics, abuse, homelessness, and anything else you might personally be struggling with and from which you want to continue to heal and help others heal. Maybe it's an eating disorder; maybe it's infertility; maybe it's fighting anxiety or depression; maybe it's mental health awareness.

Whatever you're passionate about, your passion is a power at work within you. And you are the key to bringing it into the world to enact real, sustainable change.

I believe it's our responsibility as human beings to take care of each other. I think it's our duty to care for each other when we're weak and broken. We need each other. I think that is the key (pun intended) to growing leaps and crossing the boundaries of social status, prejudice, complacency, and narcissism.

Just keep your eyes open. There are locks all around you. Maybe you hold the key to someone else's freedom.

Sometimes I think, *What if I hadn't talked to Rob and Cera that day? What if I just focused on my plans for the night (acting class) and kept walking to my car? What if I just kept pursuing my "in the box" entertainment careers and never let my creativity flow by running with the engraved key idea?* I think about the millions of people in this world who have ideas bubbling inside, just waiting to be acted upon. That untapped potential is pure gold. Why are more of us not mining for it?

What if a single mom discounts her idea because she doesn't feel she has the time or what it takes? What if the seventeen-year-old high school girl knows she's meant to stand up and be bold in the face of an injustice but doesn't think she's qualified enough? What are we missing out on in this world because people think they need to have more figured out first?

Start small. Start with what you already have. You have a birthday, correct? So for your next birthday, you can tell your family and friends to give to this cause instead of presents for you. And just like that, you will have your foundation to launch from.

Start now. Start small. Get creative.

Truly, no MBA needed. You don't need large amounts of money. As you can brilliantly learn from my naiveté, all you *really* need is a pen, a passion, a used plastic bag, and some tweezers.

So perhaps you simply need a quick trip to CVS instead of business school. (Again, I'm *not* knocking business school if that's your path—waving to my four best friends with MBAs!) I'm just asking the question. Can you put together the pieces of your story, look at your one-of-a-kind experiences and abilities, and see how your own uniqueness can guide you? You have everything you need right now to start.

It's fascinating that pounding out positive words over and over for hours can beautifully brainwash us, improving a person's well-being, hope, and motivation; how engraving words like HOPE, LOVE, and BRAVE on our scratched-up lives can give them new meaning. Each unique key holds a special purpose for each of its owners. It starts with the key engraver, and it will be passed around the world to just the right person, the person who most needs it. It's a ripple effect of hope and encouragement. And it starts with a first step. It doesn't matter if you don't know step ten or even step three of your own dream, it just matters that you start. Because we need what you have to offer. We're all in this together. We need each other. We are all part of this love movement.

If you want to do something great in the world, you might need a cash flow spreadsheet. Eventually. But do you need that right now? Can't you get started without one? (Trust me, I have one now, and I liked life better without it—much to the dismay of my CFO). But what you need even more than that is an open mind, curiosity, humility, grace, compassion, and the ability to stay with something even when it doesn't look exactly the way you dreamed.

Here's the good news: you already have everything you need inside.

Recently, as a gift, my mother framed *The Giving Tree* book cover for me, and I display it prominently in my office. It's a reminder of what it takes to live for a bigger purpose. It's a reminder to me that I don't need an MBA, that the core of what I needed to start The Giving Keys has always been with me since the days of *The Giving Tree*—snuggled up on that couch next to my mom, leaning in and begging her to turn the page.

chapter two

PLAYING UNDERCOVER

When we become aware that we do not have to escape our pains, but we can mobilize them into a common search for life, those very pains are transformed from expressions of anger into signs of hope.

—Henri Nouwen, *The Wounded Healer*

Most of us are hiding something. It might be a physical part of your body that makes you feel weak or flawed—a birthmark or deformity or cellulite or "fat" around your waist. Maybe it is your family or your upbringing or your background. It might be something you've done that makes you feel ashamed. Or maybe it was something done *to* you that you swore you'd never talk about to anyone. But what if the very thing you are hiding from the world is the thing that makes you extraordinary?

I grew up with a lot of abnormal health issues that deeply affected my identity as a girl, then as a woman. It all started in fifth grade when I became severely fatigued, so much so that I literally could not lift my head from my desk at school. On really bad days, I'd stay home from school, and my mom would spoon-feed Cheerios to me in bed because I was so weak. We knew something was wrong but couldn't figure out what it was.

You know those experiences in life that shape and define you but which you'd never wish on anyone? You don't know it when you're in the middle of it, but you look back and realize how hard and pivotal it was. Maybe you unexpectedly lost someone you loved. Maybe it was a divorce between your parents or between you and your spouse. Maybe you have a health issue like me, and you've battled it your whole life. We all have stories. Some we've carried our whole lives. Stories we've never told because the embarrassment, shame, and guilt are too overwhelming. What if these stories are the very key to our great purpose?

Well, it's time for me to lay it all out. This is my story, the one I've never fully told. It's a story about my body.

The severe fatigue continued, so my mom took me to countless doctors, who ordered all sorts of tests. They discovered it was a congenital developmental abnormality, and they discovered I had a goiter on my thyroid. I had both hypothyroidism and Hashimoto's disease; my thyroid had completely stopped working. Since this is the gland that controls hormones, adrenaline, and even major organs, including the heart, it was no wonder I was feeling so terrible. The doctors prescribed medications, which did start helping with the fatigue, but over time we realized something else was wrong. I was becoming a teenager, and while all my friends started getting their periods and developing breasts, I didn't.

Through junior high and then into high school, I still had no period. All the girls around me got their token "red balloons" at school to celebrate "becoming a woman" and it was blatantly obvious (to me, at least) that I hadn't gotten one.

First of all, that's weird, right? But it was a thing. And I found myself, day after day, waiting for my red balloons.

Maybe you're waiting to meet the right person, and it feels like everyone around you is already married. Maybe you want so badly to have children, and you just haven't been able to yet. Maybe you've had to spend time in the hospital, and you feel like you're missing out on life. If you've ever felt like you're behind, I get it. That doesn't make it better, but I get it.

We've all been teenagers, so you know how it goes. When you develop normally, you get boobs. And at this pivotal, confusing time in life, boys start to like you. When boys like you, they flirt with you, try to date you, and kiss you. I started to doubt if I'd ever get the chance to experience these moments. You know, the *real stuff* of high school. But oddly, life kept going. Still no red balloons.

So I hid in plain sight, running varsity track and playing basketball and happily landing leads in all our high school plays. (I must say, playing Sandy in *Grease* will FOREVER be the highlight of my life.) Even as all of this happened—and it wasn't all terrible—my body wasn't developing properly.

When I was seventeen, a doctor told me I had the estrogen level of a nine-year-old girl. My testosterone, on the other hand, was always through the roof. Did that mean I was somehow half girl, half boy? Why was I so different? I was so confused. My acne got so bad I went on Accutane—four times—but to no avail. Accutane is the strong stuff, the stuff that lists a million side effects, including "can cause suicidal thoughts." Perfect, just what an insecure, body-conscious teenage girl needed. But it was supposed to be the stuff that could cure anybody of acne.

Well, apparently not me.

Oh, and I probably kept Jolene Bleach in business with the amount of cream I bought to bleach the *bushes* of long, dark brown hair on my arms. Can I get an AMEN from all the ladies out there with dark body hair? Do you want to hear something *really* attractive? After I'd bleach my arm hair—so it was big and blonde and bushy instead of big and brown and bushy—a day later, I'd have roots. Yes, ARM HAIR ROOTS. You can't make this stuff up.

Oh, and because I'm certain you're wondering, I have now graduated to just shaving my arms daily. (And face.) Yes, glamorous, I know.

Meanwhile girls would complain about going to the gynecologist to get their first test "down there." They would get so worked up about how invasive it was, and that made sense. I understood because I had been having those invasive, crippling, "down there" tests for years. I was having those tests monthly, sometimes weekly. Yes, *weekly*. I felt damaged and traumatized.

The intensity of my health problems were impacting my mental and emotional health, too. To this day, I still remember in graphic detail a horrible dream I had as a teen. It was my birthday party. My family and friends were sitting at a long table at my favorite restaurant, Ed Debevic's. Everyone was dressed in 50s costumes. In this dream, my dad looked at me and said, "You're going to be messed up for the rest of your life because of what those doctors have done to you!" Then he made a graphic finger motion no man should ever make to a girl, much less a father to his daughter. On her birthday. How do you forget something like that?

Yes, it was a dream. It didn't really happen, but it's interesting what our subconscious holds on to and how it manifests itself in our daily lives. My shame ran deep. I tried everything to fix myself and feel like a feminine girl, but nothing worked. I just wanted to be normal.

I was put on all different kinds of medications to try to trigger my period. My mother even took me to a hippy acupuncturist, long before acupuncture was a common practice. He was this kooky-looking bearded man who looked exactly like the comedian Gallagher, the one who smashes watermelons. The acupuncturist would sometimes forget to take the pins out of my forehead before he asked me to turn over, and to my great dismay, the needles would smash into my face. He would also use this cigar-type incense thing that burned heavy smoke, and he waved it in voodoo-like circular motions over my ovaries.

And no, it didn't work.

My point, though, is that we tried everything.

So there I was, at eighteen, and after trying every different type of new medication, I finally got a *drop* of period. It was the most exciting thing I've ever seen in my toilet! (Yes, I said exciting.) But then, after that drop, weeks and weeks went by without another. Over the next few months, I endured episodes of excruciating pain in my lower abdomen. My mom would find me doubled over in pain on the bathroom floor. It turned out I had ovarian cysts that were bursting, which put me in the hospital multiple times. Doctors said I had polycystic ovary syndrome (and some other medical issues) that would likely keep me from being able to have children.

The doctors said the solution to the issue was birth control pills—which were not needed for anything other than regulating my period because I was the abstinence *queen* at the time—but they did finally win me the thrilling prize of a regular period. My peers would have laughed if they knew I was on the pill, since I was the least likely of all of us to have sex.

At this point you're probably thinking, *Great! She started developing properly, and the rest is history.* Except that's not exactly what happened. This is the part of the story I've never told people before—the *real* story behind why I wanted to start LoveYourFlawz. com. The whole thing has felt too vulnerable and too shameful to tell. But I know I'd be doing you a disservice if I didn't tell the rest of the story. So here goes nothing.

With all my thyroid and hormonal problems that started at age ten, I only developed one breast.

My right breast wasn't even a small A cup, and my left breast was nonexistent. In fact, it was actually a concave inversion in my chest. It looked like I had a deformed young boy's chest. All the dark arm hair, all the medications, all the invasive vaginal exams, all the mental and emotional trauma, not getting my period—all of that was bad. But there was *nothing* as bad as looking at myself in the mirror and seeing my deformity.

This has been a secret I've held inside for my entire life, and it feels like the most shameful thing I could admit. The thought of writing this to you has been absolutely mortifying (along with what's coming in chapter 9—just you wait). I've been embarrassed to tell you. It all feels a little too private. A little too TMI. Being vulnerable sounds great in theory, but it can be terrifying. Still, I knew it was time to lay it out for the sake of my healing—and hopefully yours, too.

I'm sure you have something you're hiding, just like me. You've likely experienced something that makes your skin crawl with shame and embarrassment. You might look in the mirror at your naked body, like I did, and hate yourself. If you feel like you are suffocating or drowning, I'm sharing this for you, so that you can find hope, and maybe, just maybe, start to believe—like I genuinely believe now—that your flaws are actually the very thing that can blossom into your depth, your story, your point of view, your purpose.

It's amazing how much energy we invest in trying to be "normal" when, in reality, our so-called "flaws" are what make us *extra*-ordinary and uniquely us. Those differences can help us find our true purpose, our great gift to the world. Easy to say, but tough to walk through—I know.

I remember feeling literally disgusted with my body. I couldn't even look down in the shower. My mom became friends with all the alteration shop owners in LA because they'd sew boob pads into the left side of all my clothes. Although I grew up in sunny Southern California, I never went to the beach or to any pool because we could never quite master the bathing suit padding. When I think about it now, it's probably one of the reasons I instead spent time being creative, hiding by playing different characters onstage, and writing music.

Although swimsuits never worked out, the seamstresses did manage to fill out my prom dress nicely. The problem was, I was so afraid of the opposite sex that I literally hid from my prom date. I didn't dance with him once. I just sat down in the back, pretending to casually shoot the breeze with all of my teachers—as far away from the dance floor as possible. And yes, this was my senior year of high school.

Meanwhile, my prom date, Adam (poor guy), was in fact the most handsome and coolest guy at Beverly Hills High School. And I liked him. I was just too nervous to get close to him because I was so self-conscious about my chest pads, if we dared to dance too close. And we couldn't kiss. Because if we kissed, then he might try to cop a feel. And that just could. not. happen.

So in general, to protect myself, I became the distant, sporty, funny, friend-zone, theater nerd, awkward girl. I used church youth group to hide, too. I figured it was a good, rock-solid layer of protection for me. Though I'm eternally grateful for all the beautiful values of love and service it instilled in me, looking back, I realize I was hiding behind my purity ring abstinence mentality. It was my safe place to camp out and not worry about getting caught in intimate interactions with the opposite sex. Naturally, that brings up a whole other set of issues, but I'll save that for later.

Did I mention the therapy? Because of all this, my parents took me to therapy. Unfortunately, my therapist was my parents' marriage counselor, Jack. He was a fifty-something, grey-haired man who tried to talk my fifteen-year-old self through body insecurities and boob issues. It was beyond awkward and uncomfortable, to say the least. I don't know who it was more awkward for, him or me. When I think back on it, it was probably more traumatic than therapeutic.

But back to the boobs. You probably want to know what happened. Well, doctors poked and prodded. None of them knew what to do. They recommended I go see plastic surgeons—yes, in high school. Before the doctors saw my chest, they would tell my mom they don't do breast augmentation surgery until a patient is eighteen years old. But once I disrobed and they saw what was going on, every single doctor had the exact same reaction. Their eyebrows shot up. They were taken aback and would say, "Ooooooh, I see."

After they gave me a good, uncomfortable feel, they all changed their narrative and said they would definitely operate on me before I was eighteen, "because this was a confirmed deformity." I've still never quite gotten all of their facial expressions out of my mind.

Their expressions of surprise reiterated my humiliation over and over. Their words echoed for so many years: "confirmed deformity."

That's me, I thought.

Finally, we found a female doctor who specialized in breast reconstruction, mainly for breast cancer patients. Most of the male doctors I met with recommended I just get large breast implants, assuming that's what every girl would want. But it wasn't what I wanted. I just wanted my breasts to be the same size, and I was more than happy with a small A cup. I was so grateful to have found a woman who sympathized, understood my situation, and made me feel comfortable.

I decided to wait to have surgery until the week after I graduated from high school. I had just turned eighteen.

To get the breasts to look the same size and shape, the doctor recommended putting a small implant in the deformed, inverted left side, and an almost empty implant in the right side, so they would be the same shape. I was terrified to be put under anesthesia and go into surgery, so I asked the doctor to play my favorite high school classic Christian worship music while they operated. As the anesthesia kicked in, I dozed off to the words of Jars of Clay's song "Flood."

My parents waited nervously in the waiting room for my surgery to be over. Finally, the doctor came out and said she almost had to abort the mission because she literally couldn't fit the small implant in the left side. She had discovered that the muscle and tissue were infused together, which was pulling the breast inward. But after an abnormally long process, she finally completed the surgery. I woke up groggily.

The doctors told me that when the drugs wore off, I would feel like I had been hit by a truck. They were right. Then, within a couple of weeks, I noticed that the left breast, which had been the problem during surgery, had all of a sudden changed. It was completely loose. Something had gone wrong. I went to the doctor, and she told me the implant had ruptured. The odds of this happening were extremely rare, but with how hard it had been to get the implant in, it was likely that it had been damaged during the surgery. So I had to go in for a second surgery immediately. They replaced the exploded implant on the left side with a new one.

Several weeks out from the second surgery, I seemed to be recovering well. I was desperately inching my way toward trying to feel comfortable in my own skin when something went wrong . . . *again*. The same left breast all of a sudden became rock-hard. I went back to the doctor.

She informed me that the implant had been encapsulated with scar tissue, which was apparently the result of my having had two major surgeries within a few months of each other. So although I needed surgery again in order to fix the problem, in accordance with the doctors' advice, my parents and I decided it would be best to wait a few more months to let my body have a break before my third breast surgery.

Months went by, and my left breast was still rock-hard while the new scars just seemed to get deeper and deeper. I was barely nineteen when I had my third reconstructive surgery on that same side. In order to mentally prepare for it, I had to compartmentalize and block out any memories of the first two surgeries. And it's almost unbelievable recounting this, but while I was in recovery from the third surgery, the same thing happened again. The left side again became rock-hard. At that point, I was so traumatized by all the surgeries, recurring problems, new scars, and new deformations to get used to that I gave up. I was done with surgery.

In fact, I started to feel ashamed that I'd taken the route of plastic surgery. I felt deflated that I had put myself through all this just to try to feel like a normal girl. I had ended up feeling like a cut-up, damaged freak of nature. Jealousy of every girl I saw who had "normal" boobs simmered under the surface. I so desperately wanted to finally just feel female and thought I would never be able to.

Shortly after all the surgeries, one of the worship music leaders at my church started reaching out and pursued me pretty aggressively. Everyone in the church looked up to him, and so did I. I mean, he was *that* youth group guy—the one who performed Christian rap during worship sets. Very Linkin Park. Of course, I had a huge crush on him. I had another hospital stint after a ruptured cyst and almost needed a blood transfusion (yes, half my church came to the hospital to pray over me, and he was one of them). He came in with sunflowers and as I lay there, limp in my hospital robe, it felt like we were in the movie *A Walk to Remember*, where the sick Mandy Moore was rescued by bad boy Shane West—so good! We began dating, and the whole thing felt like a fairy tale. Maybe I could be a beautiful, flirtatious, desirable woman after all.

We started recording worship duets together. I'd sing, and he'd rap over the chorus. He would leave mix tapes on my car's dashboard, which was very high school youth group of him. He'd even decorate the outside of the mix tapes with paper-mâché and Scriptures. I mean, c'mon—this was every church girl's dream guy, right here. He saved every email (and AOL chat) we ever wrote back and forth (there were hundreds) and made them into a book as thick as the Lord of the Rings trilogy for Valentine's Day. He was the first man I loved. As you can probably expect, if you've ever been young and in love, I saw my forever with him. But after two magical years together, he picked me up from the train station one day, and that's when I knew something was wrong. He drove me home, and while we sat in his grey Saab, he told me he "felt like God needed him to go through a dark tunnel right now . . . alone." He said he didn't want to bring me through the dark tunnel with him. I was just sitting there thinking, *What the hell does that mean?*

I was devastated. He said it was because "God told him to" (churchy people's most popular and most annoying way to break up with someone), which only confused me more. But then, only a month later, he proposed to his ex-girlfriend.

Knife to the heart.

Must have been a short dark tunnel, buddy.

But to make it worse—and here's why this story matters here— years later, he reached out to me to tell me that the "real" reason he broke up with me was because of my body. He proceeded to give me all the twisted details. He said the reason he was going to therapy when we were dating was because he didn't know how to justify two opposing Scriptures in the Bible and what they meant for him if he stayed with me. He quoted one Scripture in the Bible that says, "a woman who fears the Lord is to be praised," and another Scripture that says ". . . may her breasts satisfy you always."

He explained that while he thought I aligned with the first Bible verse, he was worried I wouldn't align with the second. My character was beautiful, he said. He loved all that about me. But then he said the words that still ring through my head today: "I was conflicted because I knew your breasts wouldn't satisfy me." He said this was why he ultimately didn't choose me. He told me he was trying to give us "closure" by sharing this information with me. Uh, thanks buddy. Closure for *whom*? His words didn't give me anything in the neighborhood of closure. Instead, they spun me into a deeper swirl of self-disgust.

In hindsight, I would never want to be with someone who believed that narrative about love. About women. About relationships. He came back to me years later, wanting to get back together, but thankfully I had found my strength and worth by then, so I was uninterested.

But at the time, I felt: Heartbreak. Isolation. Shame. Embarrassment. It was all so deep. The words sometimes still ring in my head. Some things never leave you. It has to become an intentional practice to not listen to the "old tapes" that sometimes rear their ugly heads. Even now, when my husband tells me that "it" doesn't bother him, it's hard to believe him. Sometimes all I can think about are those words I heard that day, the words my ex, Mr. Spiritual, said. But then I choose to quiet the voices. I choose to let go and be free.

I didn't know this back then, but what I know now—with time, good therapists, building relationships with the right people, and fighting hard—is that there is a light at the end of the dark tunnel (my dark tunnel, not his). My health issues have continued to be a burden for most of my life. I've had to fight like hell for my body, my mental health, my emotional health, and my purpose. I've had to draw from my deepest reserves of strength to believe I am beautiful just as I am. In fact, it has been the fight of my life. What I've come to believe is this: the very thing that makes you feel unlovable and incapable is the very key to unlocking your mission, your life's work, and your purpose in this world. And I hope that, now that you know my story, you'll believe I mean business when I say this.

The campaign LoveYourFlawz came out of the pain and struggle I experienced. Now I have the privilege of speaking at universities, TEDx Talks, churches, women's empowerment seminars, Girl Scout conventions, and business conferences about my journey. While we're being honest, though, I admit I've been afraid to tell the full truth about my breasts publicly. I spun the story to be about growing up with bad acne and being self-conscious, comparing myself to "perfect" women in the media. But that's changing now. It's time to lay it all out. And there's a lot more to the story, which I'll keep sharing with you. I'm done being ashamed. I'm done playing undercover. This is the real stuff. And it's the stuff of freedom.

Here's the deal: life is messy. You might not know all that you're called to yet. You might feel discouraged, worthless, or insecure about your body, your work, the life you're building. But you don't have to be perfect to have a calling. Quite the opposite, in fact. Your imperfections are talking to you. Your imperfections are your key. They can unlock all the joy, creativity, beauty, depth, vulnerability, friendship, and the life you've been waiting for.

It's our life's work to keep digging, keep searching, and keep asking God what he has for us, what he was thinking when he made us, how he wants to use us to heal others. But it's a journey that I believe begins with a daring question: what if the things you're most ashamed of, the things you most want to hide, don't have to hold you back? What if they were meant to propel you forward into your greatest purpose?

chapter three

LISTEN TO YOUR PEACE-O-METER

To make the right choices in life, you have
to get in touch with your soul. To do this,
you need to experience solitude, which most
people are afraid of, since in silence you
hear the truth and know the solutions.
—Deepak Chopra

*I*f you're ready to do the deep work of finding your unique purpose, there's one thing you can't ignore. You may call it your
intuition, your gut, God, the Universe, your "knower," your spirit,
your instinct. I call it my Peace-o-Meter. It's that still, small voice.
The feeling I have when something deep within me knows what to
do. It's about following the peace.

It can be as deep and serious as knowing you are continually
repeating unhealthy patterns in your life. Or it can be as simple as
the feeling you get when you walk out of a restaurant and something

in you says to go back inside and wait. It's when you're interviewing for a new job and things are going smoothly by all accounts, but in your heart you have a feeling something's "off," so you don't take the job. It's when you're dating the "perfect" person, but something in you feels sick to your stomach knowing they aren't right for you. It's when you feel too hopeless to go on another blind date, but something in you says, *This one is different*, and that person turns out to be your spouse. This part of you is always speaking to you. It's just that many of us aren't listening.

When I was getting The Giving Keys off the ground, I got myself into a rough situation and wished so badly that I could rewind and listen to my Peace-o-Meter. Through an acquaintance's referral (aka: I didn't know this person very well), I hired a guy—we'll call him Bill—to make the first LoveYourFlawz website. He basically did it for free, because he thought our mission was great and he had two daughters of his own. He lived in a different town, so we never met in person. We worked together via email and spoke on the phone a few times. I was happy with how the website turned out, so I hired him to make the first website for The Giving Keys as well. I'd send him pictures, copy, and drawings of how I wanted everything laid out on the new site. He followed through and built out the full vision I had in mind.

It was all happening so fast, and I was pleased and grateful.

We finally made plans so we could meet in person. I met his sweet wife and their adorable kids. On the outside, they seemed like a lovely family, but I had a little "check in my spirit," as they say. I couldn't put my finger on it, though, so I just let it be. I ignored that feeling and kept moving. We had so much to do, and we needed to keep hustling.

So Bill kept running and maintaining our website. He controlled the back end of our site where all the orders came in. As The Giving

Keys started to grow, Rob, Cera and I couldn't keep up with order fulfillment. There were so many pouring in, Bill offered to turn his garage into our inventory storage facility. Though I felt a little uneasy about this makeshift solution, I didn't think I had any other options, as we really needed the space and were growing so quickly. He began helping us fill and ship the orders to both online customers and major wholesale store accounts. We were rolling, and business was booming.

Then I heard through the grapevine that he and his wife were in the process of getting a divorce. Not only that, but she had a restraining order against him. *Deep breath.* There was that original reservation I'd had bubbling up again.

But he had become an integral part of making The Giving Keys run, and I didn't think I had time to replace him, so I convinced myself everything was fine. After all, things had been seamless with our business relationship. I hoped it would just work itself out.

Over the next few weeks and months, I continued to hear stories about Bill that concerned me, but I let it be. He was handling a whole system of our business, and he was the only one who knew how to do it. We honestly couldn't keep the business running at that pace without him. I wrestled and debated if I should fire him based solely on the creepy feeling I had. But I didn't. I kept not listening to that still, small voice. I kept staying busy. Kept thinking it would either go away or that nothing was actually wrong. Kept covering up, stifling my Peace-o-Meter. But it had been trying to tell me something all along, to warn me.

It's a teachable moment. When you know you missed it. When you know you didn't pay attention to what your heart was trying to tell you all along. Self-doubt, excuses, and fear creep in. We look outside of ourselves to what other people say or do or think and base our decisions on external influences. We feel insecure and weak, and we rely on others to make decisions.

It makes me mad thinking about how often that happens. We women sometimes doubt our ability to know. To make sound, reliable decisions for ourselves. We do it all the time. Maybe it's all the years of inequality, sexism, and patriarchy that have crept so deeply into our souls to make us doubt and even abandon ourselves.

As our little company kept growing, a few boutique store accounts contacted me saying they had never received their orders. This was unusual. I questioned Bill about it because that was his responsibility. He confirmed that the orders were mailed. But it didn't make sense to me that multiple stores were not receiving their orders, and all around the same time. My Peace-o-Meter was now shooting sparks, trying to tell me something.

Finally, we were in a financial position to get our first official office on Broadway in downtown LA. Sure, it had rats, no air conditioning, and there were frequently streaks of human feces across our front door—but it was our first real office, and we were thrilled. With our growth, I was able to hire a production manager who was skilled at handling back end operations. Sure enough, within a few weeks of hiring her, she called me, and her tone told me right away that this was serious.

"Caitlin," she said, "I think we have a fraud situation happening on the back end of our website."

Initiate heart palpitations.

It turned out Bill had created a fake account via PayPal and had been funneling every third order payment into his own separate fraud account. He'd simply added an 's' onto the fraudulent email attached to the account, so it was almost impossible to notice at a glance when looking through transactions and receipts.

I called PayPal to try to figure out what was happening, and based on what they saw, they told me to call 911 immediately. Unfortunately, the police weren't much help. They said it would be more expensive to take him to court—costing more money than he had actually taken from The Giving Keys. While we were doing well enough to pay our bills, we didn't have any extra money to burn.

I called my dad in a panic, and he set me up with one of his clients' celebrity security consultants, who was well-versed in fraud situations like mine. One of them brought me to a detective, who also told me there wasn't much I could do because it would just be so expensive to fight the case in court. When I sat in that detective's office that day, guns all over the walls, I remember thinking, *How did this tiny little giveback project I started end up bringing me here?!*

Meanwhile, as the detective went over the details of the case with me, I couldn't believe what I was hearing—which was that my best bet was to let it all go. All I could think was, *This is wrong! This guy has been committing fraud for months, we caught him, and now you expect me to let it go?!* I was angry. I felt stuck in a broken and unfair system. I felt violated. I had trusted Bill and given him so much freedom. How could he do this, especially to a company that was doing good in the world?

Then that still, small voice came back. *I tried to warn you. I tried.*

Needless to say, when all this went down, I finally parted ways with Bill. But I was still trying to figure out how much damage had been done and what to do about it. A few weeks later, I googled "The Giving Keys." The first thing that popped up was an ad for something called Charity Gift Box.

Hmm, I thought, *I've never heard of Charity Gift Box.*

That's when I saw it. In big, bold letters it read, "Discounted Giving Keys Necklaces." Faster than my fingers could click, I was already boiling with anger and dread. I clicked on the ad, and it took me to a site selling a lot of hodgepodge items (it was almost like someone trying to get rid of random things in their garage—old umbrellas, used lamps, used rain jackets). These random items took up about 10 percent of the website. The rest of the website was filled with Giving Keys images—our jewelry being sold for *half price*. As I began making sense of what I was seeing, I looked closer at the images—*our* images. But these keys were definitely *not* giving back to our mission. I remembered the way Bill used to tie the leather and suede onto the keys. He didn't do it the way I wanted, so I had to coach him to make the ties properly.

The photos on Charity Gift Box's site were tied the way I hated . . . *the way Bill did it.*

In that moment, I became my own detective. I put together the pieces of what I was discovering. He had created this website and was making the jewelry himself, but he was marketing it as if it was authentic Giving Keys product. I was both fuming and panicking. I couldn't believe what I had just found. I had lost faith in going the police route, though, so I decided I had to figure this out on my own.

I sat on it for a few days in order to calm down and gather my thoughts. Then I had an idea. I decided to bulk text Bill, along with ten other numbers he didn't know, and write, "Bill, I am putting you on this bulk text message with police officers, detectives, pastors, and lawyers. You must cease and desist Charity Gift Box immediately, or I will press charges, and all of the people on this text message will come after you to protect The Giving Keys."

Please note that I didn't know what "cease and desist" fully meant, except what I'd learned by googling it five minutes before I sent the text. But it sounded right and threatening enough. Please also bless with me my ride-or-die family and friends, who gave their permission to be part of this stunt.

Bill, of course, had no idea the ten people on that text message were actually my mom, dad, sister, brother, and friends posing as elite legal enforcement to scare him.

Five minutes after I sent the text, he wrote back, "It's down."

Victory! I felt like James Bond, babe version. My bluffing threat had worked. My friends started telling me my life had turned into a *CSI* episode. They were kind of right.

I won the part where the fraud Charity Gift Box site got taken down, but Bill still stole thousands of dollars from The Giving Keys. During this fiasco, it was impossible to pay our employees and the rent on our new office space. This was one of our *many* low points. I couldn't believe I had allowed myself to be so dependent on someone so unworthy of my trust. I couldn't believe how right my Peace-o-Meter had been from the beginning.

Thankfully, during this time, my parents loaned me some money to cover the office rent and payroll. I would need to pay them back, of course, but I had no long-term sustainable plan to turn the ship back around. I was feeling extremely desperate, and the only reason I didn't give up was that the still, small voice inside of me told me this wasn't going to be the end of The Giving Keys. This movement was a God-sent idea, and it was changing people's lives. I knew it had to keep going, so I was determined to fight the injustice and make it to the other side. The Giving Keys was going to be healthy and run successfully again. We had a mission to spread around the world.

Determination is one thing. But the reality of picking up the pieces and putting them back together was another.

A couple months passed, and I was still trying to get The Giving Keys back on its feet. I had heard about this great gospel church called One Church, and one Sunday, I asked my roommate at the time (who was a Buddhist) if she would go with me to check it out. She agreed.

We didn't know anyone. We just sat in the middle of the crowd, taking it all in. The music was incredible, and Pastor Touré Roberts (who I'd never met or heard preach before) started his sermon, and I was impressed right from the start. Then, out of the blue, right in the middle of his sermon, something totally unexpected happened. He stopped in his tracks, looked out into the audience, and hesitated before opening his mouth again:

"I feel like I'm supposed to stop what I'm talking about and say this. I feel like there's someone in here who started a business, and it was successful. Right now you're going through a storm, and you think that you maybe need a partner to get you through the storm. But God wants me to tell you, you don't need this partner. You don't need a partner because God will be your partner. He will get you through the storm."

Of course, I thought to myself, *That could be about me*, but then I quickly talked myself out of it. What are the odds that at this random church, on this random Sunday morning, God would speak through a random pastor to give a message to me?

Then my Buddhist roommate elbowed me, and said, "Hey, I think he's talking to you." It was a fair thought. I had been thinking about bringing in a partner to help me with The Giving Keys. I hadn't taken any steps in that direction but had thought about how much easier it would be if I didn't have to constantly put out fires all by myself. That alone could have been confirmation enough, but I realized my Peace-o-Meter was going off. It all felt right. After several minutes of letting it fully sink in, I thought to myself, *I think that was for me.*

I walked out of One Church on a high of joyful, peaceful excitement. My heart believed it, but honestly, my mind was still trying to make excuses about how it wasn't real or for me. My mind wanted to protect my heart from being too easily swayed or spiritually manipulated. I'd been there before. I didn't want to believe a "word from God" that could just be a preacher's emotion or opinion. But then again, even my Buddhist roommate thought it was for me.

I let it sit in the back of my mind all day, and I felt hopeful for the first time in months.

Later the same day, I met up with my ex-boyfriend (yes, the "I can't marry you because of the Scripture about boobs" ex-boyfriend). He was in town from New York and had asked if I wanted to grab dinner with him. I was thirty at the time, still single, and probably a little desperate. I admit the thought occurred to me that maybe he regretted his younger years boob POV, and maybe sparks would fly again like a twisted version of *The Notebook*.

On top of everything else, he had an MBA and was the vice president of a big venture capital firm in New York.

So we had dinner, and, over glasses of wine and pasta dishes, he proposed a $20,000 investment in The Giving Keys to be able to pay my employees, cover operational expenses, and help sustain us. I couldn't believe it. This was the help I'd been looking for—delivered right to my doorstep. Wasn't it?

I was flattered and shocked. I sat there, staring at my pasta dish, trying to think of a reason—any reason—to turn down this generous offer. That's when he said it.

"Caitlin, you're a creative genius, but you're kind of like Dennis the Menace when it comes to business. I can help you run a *true business*."

He told me I shouldn't have to deal with the day-to-day operations, and that he could easily run the business side of things and fund us. Then he said the magic words—the words I'd been waiting for, without even knowing it.

"We would be partners."

My jaw dropped. Then I smiled. Literally just hours earlier, that pastor had told me God said *I didn't need a partner.* Just hours ago. I desperately needed the financing, and the offer was incredibly tempting.

"So what do you think?" he asked.

I paused.

"Wow," I said. "I'm incredibly flattered, but no."

He kept trying to persuade me. I could tell he was genuinely shocked and disappointed that I didn't want his help. But I knew deep down in my "knower," my Peace-o-Meter, that it was the right decision. I knew I was meant to be at that church that Sunday to hear that word, and that it was indeed meant for me.

A week or so later, I got a call from a friend of a friend who was hosting a big faith leadership conference in Atlanta. They wanted to bring in and feature a few giveback brands and give us a chance to sell product, too. They wanted each product to be sold for twenty dollars, and although we normally sold our jewelry for more, I decided to go. There were fifteen thousand people planning to attend the conference, and they told each giveback brand to bring a thousand products. The conference's goal was to get the audience to buy enough product to sell out our inventory.

During the conference, they showed a video about The Giving Keys, and from that point on, we sold nonstop for two days straight. We sold out of the one thousand pieces. And here's the best part. Have you figured out the dollar amount of our sales for those two days? $20,000. The *exact same amount* my ex-boyfriend had offered to invest if I made him a partner.

Fast forward to today: I'm married with children, and THANK

GOD I'm not business partners with my ex-boyfriend! Peace-o-Meter for the win.

This Peace-o-Meter is something I believe we all have. But you have to cultivate it. Practice, almost. You have to learn how to hear it, listen to it, sense it, and know it. Whatever you want to call it—God, the Universe, your gut—you have to pay attention, or you could miss it: your purpose, your calling, the reason you're here, and what you have to offer.

I've had some big misses with my Peace-o-Meter, but the failures have just encouraged me to pay attention to it more.

You can learn to sense it in all kinds of situations. Like when you know deep down that your fiancé is not right for you. Or when you have a feeling you can't trust a friend, lover, family member, employee, or partner. Or the instinct to set stronger boundaries in your life to help you find more time for self-care. Or a talent, passion, idea, or dream that has been lying dormant inside you, and you know you have to do something with it. Your Peace-o-Meter can guide you no matter what question you're trying to answer, but you have to learn how to listen.

How can you know if your Peace-o-Meter is trying to tell you something? It has at least one signature that's easy to spot: it will always prioritize wisdom for the long-term over what you want in that moment.

All this said, I have to add something more: sometimes you will be torn and confused. You'll battle at times to identify where the peace is, but I believe if you slow down and prayerfully ask for direction and discernment, things will open up, start to unfold, and become clear. Start listening for the small nudges, and soon you'll be able to recognize the Peace-o-Meter in your big choices as well.

After the Bill fail, our Giving Keys production manager was overwhelmed with the mess of it all, and one day, as I was walking out the door with my hands full of heavy displays for an event, she held the door open for me and said she needed to quit. I didn't blame her. I dropped everything and texted a few friends to see if they knew anyone who would be interested in being a production manager, making basically no money and with no health benefits. We were in pre-start-up mode, not sexy start-up mode.

I had a friend, Brit Gilmore, who worked in fashion but also had a heart for giving back. Since she already had a legitimate career with stock options, I didn't think she would be interested in my scrappy start-up, but she was moved by the mission, as she'd always had a dream to marry fashion and philanthropy. We both felt peace that she would be a beautiful addition to our mission. She became our production manager, which turned into her redoing our website, which turned into her becoming our president, which turned into her being on a Times Square billboard for Shinola featuring the work she's done at The Giving Keys, which turned into her making the highly reputable and coveted *Forbes* 30 Under 30 list for her work at The Giving Keys. She was a godsend.

But back then, we still had to pick up the pieces. I'm forever grateful for Brit and my team because it turned out we could do so in good company, together.

Just as your Peace-o-Meter knows when something is wrong, it also knows when something is *right*. We can learn to listen to its red alerts *and* its green lights.

Recently I did a podcast interview with an inspiring singer, Andy Grammer (he sings one of my favorite anthems, "Keep Your Head Up"). He asked me, "Why do you think The Giving Keys succeeded when perhaps others who have tried to start giveback brands have not?" I replied that for me, it came down to following this inner knowing, this feeling I had deep within me that it was a green-light opportunity.

By "green light," I mean the opportunity was bright enough for me to stay up all night working on it; giving up was not an option. It was something I *had* to keep doing. I listened to the still, small voice that told me not to settle when I was waiting for the missing link to make it about more than passing along keys with words on them. The voice that helped me identify the opportunity to start employing people transitioning out of homelessness, which gave us a double differentiating factor and set us apart in the industry. Both factors made customers and stores fall in love with us. If they weren't going to fall in love with one side of our mission, they'd fall in love with the other.

Then Andy asked, "What was your most recent situation or encounter where you felt that direction and clarity from the divine?"

I wasn't expecting that question. I was taken aback a little and paused to think. I felt sad to say that I actually hadn't had a divine encounter in a long time. I went on to say that maybe it was because I wasn't sowing into my spiritual side as much as I probably could or should. But the question stayed with me after I left the interview.

To my surprise, the very next day, I experienced what Andy called a "clarity from the divine" moment.

I went to a session with my old therapist, Ann, and at the very end of the session, Ann told me it's my life's work to not fall into being fearful. To look for synchronicity. To look for those little "God Taps," the "breadcrumbs" God gives us to follow as a way of reassuring us he's with us. We don't need to live in fear. For me, Ann said, it was all about not letting fear run my life. Don't let fear win.

Just as we were getting up to say goodbye, I looked down at

my phone and saw I had a text from my sister-in-law, Kenda. She knew I had been struggling with discipline and sleep issues with my two-year-old son, Brave.

Her text said this: "Hi sis! I listened to this message from pastor Judah Smith today, and it was really great about endurance and facing fears. I think that's something you are facing with Brave. The uphill daily battles with him require endurance and I thought this would give you some inspiration. Love you. XO."

Judah is the pastor of a church in LA, and the title of the sermon Kenda sent me was "Facing the Future without Fear." Immediately, I ran back into the therapist's room and said, "Wow, you just mentioned synchronicity and how we need to pay attention to the little God Taps, and I just now got this text from my sister-in-law talking about exactly what you encouraged me to work on!"

It was a little moment but a big moment. It was a breadcrumb that I was on the right track.

Right after my session with the therapist, I wanted to go downstairs to this little retail shop below Ann's office because, from the outside, a baby onesie had caught my eye. It had words in French that I couldn't quite make out, though I did see a line that said the word "miracle." Right under the words was an image of an eye. I asked the store owner what the phrase meant.

She said, "It actually means *You are a miracle*."

Of course, I bought the onesie as well as the wall art to match. I was six months pregnant with a little girl. I had waited my whole life for her, but I hadn't bought even one thing for her yet. Nothing had felt quite special enough. *This* was the first thing I'd ever buy her. A little token I'd always remember. Perfect.

Driving home, I sent a voice memo to Kenda, my sister-in-law, telling her how much her text meant to me and what perfect timing it was. I told her I hadn't even listened to the sermon yet, but her text and the timing was so serendipitous with my therapy session and my podcast with Andy Grammer that I just wanted to say thanks. She responded that she actually rarely listens to sermons, much less sends them to people. But that day she happened to be listening while she was doing laundry and felt "in her spirit" that she was supposed to send it to me.

Thankfully, she must've been listening to her Peace-o-Meter, too. You'll never believe what she said next.

She said, "You are a miracle, Caitlin. And Brave is a miracle."

My jaw dropped.

"Wait, what?! What?! What?! What?! What?!" I said out loud, looking down at the onesie and artwork I had just bought.

This was way more than a "God breadcrumb." It was a fresh-from-the-oven God-brioche-loaf-with-melted-butter—warm, gooey, and heavenly.

It was like God knew about my conversation with Andy the day before. Like he was paying attention to my one little life and cared. That moment of synchronicity comforted me.

In case you're feeling lost or alone right now, I want to remind you that you are being guided, whether you can feel it right now or not. Whether you hear it right now or not. The Spirit who guides us is a loving one who has our best interests in mind. Sometimes we just need to slow down enough to tune in and listen.

Like yoga instructor Adriene Mischler says, "The wind of grace is always blowing. Set your sail to catch it."

It's so easy to spend your life looking outside yourself in order to know what to do next. But what would your life look like if you started trusting what's inside you? Believe you have what it takes to move through your life. It is your life, after all.

~

It's important to listen to your Peace-o-Meter for *so many* reasons, but the main reason is that literally nobody else in the world can know your purpose like you can. Don't get me wrong; it's beneficial and wise to seek external advice and opinions at times. That's why I seek business advice from experts in finance and human resources. That's why I sometimes see a therapist. But when it comes to your purpose—the great gift you alone have to give to the world—you're the only one who can know deep down if you're doing it.

In fact, if all you're doing is listening to the advice of others, you'll miss it. They know *their* purpose, not yours.

Perhaps there's more joy, peace, and contentment for you. Only *you* know if there's a hole to fill deep in your soul. Trust yourself.

If you're still not sure, when choosing your path, look for these fruits: peace of mind, gratification, and a knowingness that your purpose could make a difference in someone's life. Look for the things that keep coming back around in your life. Especially when it's something you've possibly given up on, laid down, or surrendered, but it keeps popping back up, there might still be something there. And if you've let the idea or dream die in its old form, it can come back around with new fresh life.

One thing you could also try is to write a list of things that bring you joy. As you do it, try to stay away from an accomplishment mentality like "get a promotion or raise" or "get some recognition or award." Try to make the list more about things that make you *feel alive*. Where and when do you feel the most like yourself?

I'll also suggest making a . . . *drum roll, please* . . . yes, a vision board. I know, I know, you're not in elementary school anymore, but this one is for adults. RAD adults. Here we go again with another handy trip to my favorite place on earth: CVS, coming in for the win to solve all of life's obstacles. Buy a few magazines that cover the bases of lifestyle, business, and any other magazines that intrigue you. Grab a poster board, scissors, and a glue stick. Pretend you won the lottery and can do anything you want: travel, study, eat, explore anywhere, and meet anyone you want. Yes, Oprah was on my vision board, and I met her, so that proves it works, people. Cut out and glue onto the poster board everything that sparks joy (as Marie Kondo would say). Then, after you're done, step back and look for the common thread. Trust me; you'll see it. And now you know what to fight for more of in your life.

Identify what's life-giving to you and put more of that in your life. And don't apologize for doing it. Don't ask for permission. What could be more important than doing what you were created for?

Here's the other thing: trust yourself. When people try to "counsel" you—even people you trust—it's OK to disagree or say "No thanks." Especially if they're pushing their beliefs or opinions on you. People sometimes want to project their solutions onto other people's problems, but you don't have to take their solutions if they're not resonating with you.

Thomas Merton said it is actually *dangerous* to put the Scriptures in the hands of people whose inner selves are not yet sufficiently awakened to encounter the Spirit, because they will try to use God for their own egocentric purposes. This is partly why some religious leaders and religion in general can become corrupt and dangerous. Trust your heart to guide you if something feels off. You might not always "feel" it, but you're strong. Give yourself the benefit of the doubt. Believe in your ability to take responsibility for your life, decisions, dreams, and future.

Can you learn to listen to your Peace-o-Meter? Can you pay attention to your body, your breath, your instinct, and your gut? I believe you have it in you. Yes, it takes practice. It takes intentionality.

You're going to miss it sometimes, but then you're going to hear it more and more easily. And when that happens, I believe you're going to be living into your purpose more often. I believe you're going to see things more clearly. I believe you're going to grow and have a positive impact on the world. Because you're the only you, and you're the only one who knows what you need most.

Okay. Now that that's done, who's ready for some warm, buttered brioche?

chapter four

A MAN'S WORLD

There are three things we have to let go of.
The first is the compulsion to be successful.
Second is the compulsion to be right—especially
theologically right. Finally, there is the compulsion
to be powerful, to have everything under control.
—Richard Rohr

*I*t feels important to say that sometimes you go hard after a dream you thought was meant for you, and it doesn't turn out the way you expected. Sometimes you walk down a long, meandering path only to find that the "gold" you were looking for at the end of the rainbow simply isn't there. You might find, when you're standing in this place, that you're tempted to think the journey has been a mistake or a waste of time. But eventually, you realize that often, what seemed like a detour was the exact path you needed in order to uncover your own miraculous and unexpected purpose— that every road we walk is shaping us into the beautiful us we were always meant to become.

Now, I'm not just talking about a dream in the childhood sense of the word, or even in the individual sense of the word, in which your "dream" is just another name for the life you want. The dreams I'm talking about are dreams of urgency because they bring meaning to your life and to the lives of others.

Think of Martin Luther King Jr.'s dream. He famously said in a speech, "I have a dream that my four little children will one day live in a nation where they will not be judged by the color of their skin, but by the content of their character." This dream wasn't just about him. It wasn't a response to the question, "What do you want to be when you grow up?" either. The dream he talked about was greater, addressing the question, "What injustice do you want to fight?"

Maybe there is a passion, pull, or dream that's been there since you were young. Maybe your dreams have changed and evolved as you've grown, but no matter what stage of life you're in, I know you have some sort of a dream in you. And when the world—or even your experience—tells you that you can't; or that it doesn't make sense; or that it's not worth it; or that it's too extreme, far-fetched, or difficult; or that you don't fit the mold—you can do this. Whatever it is your soul is whispering to you, I want you to run after it with all your strength.

And remember, when it seems like your dream has let you down, it may just need to be rearranged, reimagined, and re-purposed—like an antique key that is passed on and on, you can count on your dream to make it where it's meant to go.

This is not an accident. None of it.

When I was seventeen, Kiss FM, the most popular radio station in LA, held musical auditions to discover the three lucky new members of the next hot girl group. Mind you, this was when Destiny's

Child, Backstreet Boys, and NSYNC were my *everything*. So naturally, I signed up immediately.

The Beverly Hills High School theater department, which I was part of, even posted the audition flyers for the competition. There was a line around the block of hundreds of girls and their mothers prepping their songs and dance routines. As for me, I had a song semi-prepared. My plan was to sing along with a song from one of my church friend's demo tapes, to which I kind of knew the words. Compelling, right? I had no dance routine prepared because I'm the worst dancer you have ever seen. (True story: years later, I was cast in a commercial as the "bad dancer version of Britney Spears.") Knowing all of this, you might be cringing a little, wondering, "Caitlin, what were you thinking?" I guess I was thinking I could make up for my fairly dramatic deficiencies by wooing them with my personality.

Needless to say, it was ambitious.

The audition line ran through the alley behind one of my favorite restaurants, Kate Mantilini. They made the best key lime pie in town. So given my well-intentioned teenage evangelist's heart, instead of preparing for the audition, I decided to buy a huge pie, have it cut into dozens of tiny pieces, and pass out slices to the girls in line, along with invitation fliers for my church youth group. My best guess is that I was *both* trying to be a "good Christian girl" as well as to distract myself from the fact that I was dramatically under-prepared.

When it was finally my turn to audition, I told them I didn't have a dance prepared, so the producer turned on some music and asked me to freestyle dance, which I did. And let me just do you a favor and paint you a picture of what my freestyle dance looked like: me hula hooping with no hula hoop, both arms straight up, turning in circles over and over. That's literally all I did the entire time. The same move during the entire song. I'm delighted nobody captured this on film.

What's interesting is that after all of my fumbling, not practicing, and pie-feeding evangelism—not to mention the hundreds of girls who auditioned—guess who made the cut? You guessed right. Imperfect *moi*.

Can we stop and talk about how sometimes you do everything wrong, you come unprepared and buy everyone pie in a back alley instead of rehearsing, and for some reason, you still get a wave of grace? A door flies open. An opportunity is granted. I want you to trust that your path is being unfolded in front of you. There are so many steps in the process for which we simply cannot take credit. I can promise you one thing: it wasn't my dancing skills that won me that audition.

Of course, sometimes it goes the other way. (Please remember this the next time you *don't* get an opportunity you wanted.) On the path to your purpose, there will be doors that "should" open for you but won't, and there will be plenty of others that should never in a million years open for you, yet they will. *This is still your path.* You haven't done anything wrong. There are so many things in life over which we simply don't have control.

At the end of the auditions, the producers selected three girls. I was one of them. I was about to spend some of the most influential years of my life (ages 17–21) being a real, full-time musician. This five-year journey would become a collage of some of the best, most disturbing, and most impactful memories of my life. That's what pursuing a dream looks like. You jump all-in and run hard. You deal with the bad and the ugly, and you try to soak in the good. The whole thing shapes and molds you. It's all part of the process. Every bit of it.

And sometimes, if you're lucky, your bad dance moves won't hold you back.

I'm sure you're all just *dying* to know the band name. OK. First we were Blush (I had a whispering part on a song intro. I whispered, "Do I make you Blush?"). Then our name changed to Daddy's Girls (cringe), and finally we were Foxi Nova. Yes, Foxi with an "i," thank you very much.

From the band name to writing songs to meeting and working with some incredibly famous producers and artists, it was a whirlwind from the very beginning. Our producer started recording our demos and showcasing them for all the different record labels, which led us to the legendary Kenny "Babyface" Edmonds. Babyface signed us to his label with Arista Records. He has written and produced albums for countless iconic artists—everyone from Whitney Houston to Mariah Carey to Pink to Eric Clapton. It was a big deal to sign with Arista Records at that time.

We started writing with Babyface, and he became a huge influence on my career—in music and beyond. We worked with him almost every day for years. Even though I already played the guitar and knew how to write songs on a natural, elementary level, he's the one who really mentored me to challenge myself to greatness, to strive to be the best writer possible. He pushed me to make lines more powerful. He'd say, "Let's find a way to make that more clever." That word, *clever*, stuck with me every time I wrote a song over the next ten-plus years. I'd get it on paper, but then keep looking at the line again and again to see if I could make it more unique and special.

He brought in some legendary musicians for us to work with (even Bob Marley's guitar player), and we had the time of our lives experiencing such brilliant musicianship and working behind the scenes with all of the greats. I even got to work with The Beach Boys' Brian Wilson, recording his demos with him. He taught me the harmonies so quickly, it was a feat to keep up with his brilliance. It was an honor to get to work so closely with such a legend.

The actual *making* of the music was a dream. But there was so much more that came with the gig than just the music.

We were scheduled to take voice and dance lessons and meet with a personal trainer every day. We were the "golden" children in all the best and worst ways. Anything we wanted or needed was at our fingertips, but also, because so much was being invested in our success, we became like commodities in a way. People who had no business caring about our bodies or how "sexy" we were (or weren't) suddenly became *very* concerned with these things.

Certain record label executives, producers, and managers started to be concerned about us gaining weight. We were all still teenagers, and also naturally thin, yet we were told to write down every single thing we ate all day in a food journal. We had to turn in our food journals to the team so they could keep tabs on us and what we were eating.

I have a video from my eighteenth birthday party, where I was eating french fries like any normal teenager would, and our tour manager held up a fork in my direction and made a stabbing motion toward me. With his face all twisted and serious he seethed, "Pick up one more fry. I dare you."

Carefully, I took the fry out of my mouth and put it back in the basket where it had come from. He dropped his fork back to his plate when I did that, and we both sat in silence for a minute before he spoke again.

Then he said, "Did you fall and hit your head and forget you were in Foxi Nova?"

Hardly a practice or routine went by when someone from our team wouldn't say things like, "Caitlin, come on! You gotta be more sexy!"

Let me just say this: if you want to give a grown woman issues with her adult sexuality, start telling her over and over again at age seventeen that she "needs to be more sexy."

Here I was, a one-boobed virgin teenager teaching Sunday school, deathly afraid of boys, and I'm supposed to . . . what? Thrust my hips or something? I quite literally didn't know how to move in a sensual way. Picture me awkwardly trying to squint my eyes, thinking, "I think this is how you look sexy?" when, in reality, it probably just looked like I had something in my eye. All in front of a bunch of grown men who were scrutinizing my every move.

Thanks to some bold souls speaking up in the media of late, I think situations like this are changing for women in entertainment and everywhere. As I put these memories down on paper, I hope the absurdity speaks for itself.

Every night we'd go out to the coolest, most exclusive clubs. Yes, we were underage, but our "team" always got us in. They wanted us to be seen "in the scene" because it was good PR. So they would usher us in ahead of the long lines. There were nights we ended up in places I never would have imagined, hanging out with some of the top stars of our day. It was glamorous, and yet the weight of unhealthy industry standards was slowly crushing me.

While entertainment seems to be a special kind of incubator for comparison and sexism and thinking of ourselves as commodities, we all have our own version of this. We look at our seemingly perfect neighbors and online "friends," we compromise our values for a paycheck, or keep our mouths shut even when we see something wrong (or when we just REALLY want a freaking french fry). It's easy to get caught up in the whirlwind and miss what our souls are whispering to us all along. They're always calling us back to our true identity and purpose.

While my new scene was all fame, sex, money, and beauty, I was still an avid rule-follower and a Sunday School teacher. So while we were being ushered into these exclusive clubs, I would usually spend the evening (while everyone else was drinking and dancing) carrying around a water bottle and ending up in the bathroom talking to and praying with girls who were drunk or having a bad night and needed a shoulder to cry on. Sometimes I'd even bring them home with me and then, of course, take them to church with me the next day, albeit hungover. Now I see that as semi-psycho of me, but bless my little heart.

No matter where you put me, *The Giving Tree* was always there.

I lived with the other girls in the group, Alaina and Christine, in a West Hollywood house. They were known/labeled as the J. Lo and Britney Spears of the group, and I was labeled as the Sheryl Crow of the group. Every guy, every celebrity in our orbit, had the biggest crush on them. There were nights when the girls had guys in their rooms, and I was awkwardly closed off in my room alone, in bed, cuddling with one of the guy's dogs (a pit bull named Broccoli was my favorite spooning partner).

As I'm sure you can imagine, in many ways I didn't feel like a normal teenager. I wanted to be a good person, to bring hope to the hopeless, and I was proud of that. But I also felt so behind in my journey to "real" womanhood, and I wondered what was wrong with me. You can imagine why I felt self-conscious when I lived with and did everything with "J. Lo" and "Britney Spears."

I was young, trying to figure out who I was and conflicted by all the different voices and opinions about who I should be.

It's not lost on me that the voices surrounding me were predominantly male. Entertainment is a male-dominated industry (not unlike many other industries in our world) which meant nearly all the individuals telling me who I should be and what I should look like and act like were men. Don't get me wrong here; I'm not anti-men. I'm married to a man I love and raising a son I adore. But this was one of the first experiences that showed me some people think women are still just living in a man's world—and this reminded me that despite the many people telling me who I should be, there was one voice that mattered most: *my own.*

If you're a woman, I want to talk directly to you for a minute. There are going to be plenty of people in the world who, although perhaps well-intentioned, are going to want to tell you who you are, what your purpose is, and what you're going to have to do to get there. You must flirt with your boss to please him or get ahead. You must be subversive and cold to your female counterparts to make sure you're the winner. You must not think there's room enough for everyone to win in their own lane. Be more sexy! Lose more weight! Be softer. Be more direct. Talk less. Talk more. Stand up. Sit down.

Why would you trust your purpose and your voice and your path to someone who couldn't possibly know the call of your soul?

Here's the truth: Your path to purpose will be lined with people shouting their opinions of which way you should go, and a lot of it will be bad advice. There will always be people who think they know better than you. Not only people who try to profit from you and who see you as a means to their own end, but even well-intentioned people like mentors, leaders, or pastors who think they know best or think they are hearing from God. This can get twisted and even dangerous if the other person is not a truly trust-worthy source confirming something you already know deep down. Remember that you do not have to listen, you do not have to stay, you do not have to take on the direction or identity someone tries to give you. You get to decide when to stay and when to go.

And no matter what, know that you get to decide who you are. You are a miracle. My daughter's onesie says so.

I fought the good fight the entire way through my years in Foxi Nova. They continued to pitch us songs that were about pushing the envelope and bending all the rules, and I continued to write songs about issues I was passionate about, such as existential questions about life; God; why drinking, drugs, and money won't fulfill anyone; and homelessness.

Every record label's dream, right?

When I found out one of the girls was having an affair with our manager, it was clear things were unraveling, and ultimately, I decided to leave the group. After five colorful, adventurous, and challenging years, I felt my inner "Peace-o-Meter" telling me it was time to move on. I always tell people, "When it's time to go, you'll know." You will feel it in your gut. As for me, when the Foxi Nova season was over, part of me was relieved and the other part felt like I was experiencing the death of a dream.

Sometimes, though, we have to let go of a small dream to get to the big one. Sometimes we have to let a dream break so we can put the pieces back together again—and it turns out even more beautiful the second time.

Life post-Foxi Nova was a lot different.

Depending on where I got traction, that's where my energy went. I would swap my attention back and forth between college, acting, and recording my own songs. Life was good, but I was hustling, hoping and praying I'd "catch a break."

In school, I majored in philosophy and minored in sociology. I was always fascinated about our existence, the point of life, and why humans do what they do. I didn't necessarily think I'd have an actual career in either field, but followed my interest in them anyway, hoping it would pay off in some way.

It was so refreshing to learn about broader topics and issues in life rather than my previous daily work of trying to write a hit song and, of course, "Be more sexy." I still wrote music for therapeutic reasons and kept in touch with Babyface, and after sharing a few of my new songs with him, I ended up signing with him as a solo artist. Maybe my dream of being a musician wasn't dead after all? A girl could hope.

One of the songs I wrote and recorded with Babyface during that time did a good job of expressing the tension of that season. It's called "Finding Feelings":

I used to practice what I
Believed but now I'm falling down
It crept up on me while I
Was sleeping softly, surprise
Gravity took a hold of me
I did not like the way you
Pushed yourself on me like a
Hurricane that came crashing down
Though I did not try to stop
The many changes I clocked
I did not have a hold of me
I know it's time to wake up
'Cause it hurts too much to make up
The colors that just make me real
I'm finally finding feelings
That remind me of the girl I used to be

In 2008, I released my first real album, *Flawz*. I wrote every single word of every single song myself. In the music industry, it's common for artists to cowrite songs, but inspiration would always strike late at night, when I was alone and without the pressure of being in a writing session with other writers, where I didn't feel comfortable or free. With my album release came my first music and radio tours. I was on cloud nine. I was touring as a solo artist, singing my own songs, and getting the chance to share my soul with the world.

Touring wasn't glamorous—I basically lived in a van full of smelly band guys—but I loved it. We ate breakfast, lunch, and dinner from drive-throughs and gas stations. (Perhaps this is where I developed my strange and vibrant love affair with gas station food snacks, which is still alive to this day.) Give me some Funyuns and Doritos any day of the week, and I'm a happy camper.

After our shows, around midnight and usually in the middle of nowhere, we would search Priceline to find the nearest, cheapest hotel. You can only imagine some of the accommodations we ended up staying in. Hotel rooms that smelled like old, rotted, grandpa cigarette smoke. But oddly enough, despite all the roughing it, I had the time of my life. I was doing it. Sometimes God gives us grace for the mud we trudge through on the path to our purpose.

I was thrilled to get some moderate success with my single "Still Have My Heart." Friends all over the country wrote to say they heard my song on the radio, which was invigorating. Sadly, it still never turned into a major hit the way my label, manager, and I expected.

They had invested so much money in me. My manager even sold his farm because he believed in me so much, but it never ended up paying off financially for anyone. I felt guilty about all of it, and yet there was nothing I could do that I wasn't already doing.

I remember calling my boyfriend at the time from one of those rough hotel rooms on tour. Through tears, I told him I'd poured out my heart, put everything into it, and it just didn't do what we all thought it was going to do. What would I do next?

How many times have you walked a path and thought to yourself, *This is it!*, only to watch it all fall apart?

When my last music tour for that particular album ended, I turned back to acting. My music agency, Paradigm, had an acting department and they sent me on one audition for a series regular role on an MTV show I ended up booking. After that finished filming, I had a big audition for Michael Patrick King's new NBC TV show pilot, *A Mann's World*. Michael is best known for being the writer, director, and executive producer of the *Sex and the City* TV show and movie. He is a brilliant, fabulous, creative genius. I grew up loving *Sex and the City*. (Ironic, I know, because I was having no sex in no cities, but I was taking notes.)

So I did my first audition with the casting director, and apparently it went well, because I got a callback to audition for Michael Patrick King himself. I could barely contain myself. You're not supposed to touch people in the audition rooms (this is pretty basic), much less attack them with an aggressive hug, but I couldn't help myself. I ran into the room and hugged him like he was my long-lost best friend. Faux pas or not, I nailed the audition.

He laughed the whole time, and later that day, I got a call that he wanted me to test for the role in front of the whole NBC Universal executive network team. Being asked to do this means it's getting serious. Your agents and attorneys start to compile the contract and negotiate your rate for not only the pilot episode but also the following seasons.

We had a few work sessions with Michael Patrick King coaching and preparing the final three girls it was down to, then I was up. I walked into a movie theater room filled with men in suits. I went straight to the front of the theater and performed the scenes. I left feeling pretty confident (which, 99 percent of the time, I do *not* feel when I leave auditions where I'm being judged from head to toe).

But then I waited.

Until eventually, I got the call that I booked the role. I was over the moon. This was really it. My life was about to change. I was going to be a lead character on a brand-new NBC show. This was a *dream*. I felt I finally would be worthy of the love and adoration of my father since I was now in the ring with all of his successful clients.

The lead actor was the legendary Don Johnson (Dakota Johnson's dad—hello *Miami Vice*), and the show was about him owning and running a West Hollywood hair salon. The show also starred the incredible Ellen Barkin.

I was one of the other leads, alongside heartthrob (and Lady Gaga's real-life fiancé) Taylor Kinney, who was my love interest on the show. They sent us to a fabulous salon in Beverly Hills to have Blake Lively's celebrity hair stylist do all of the cast members' hair. My hair was colored maroon for the role. We had fittings and got all of our wardrobe made by the incomparable Patricia Fields (who is famous for all of the *Sex and the City* costumes). I was literally living in my dream world.

We filmed on the NBC studio lots for about a month, recorded promotional videos, and even took pictures that were set to be on buses and billboards promoting the release of the show.

That's when I got the call. The night before I was supposed to fly to New York City for the event that would kick off the press for the show, my agent called and told me NBC had decided not to pick up the show. *The Voice* had just aired and was such a major success for the network, they were going to bump our show and give *The Voice* a two-hour slot, instead of one hour. Our cast and crew were all shocked.

Now I suddenly had an open schedule, a more-than-slightly-broken heart, and a small side project I was working on that had to do with some old, rusty keys.

chapter five

THE SURPRISE OF SURRENDER

For broken dreams, the cure is,
dream again and deeper . . .
—C. S. Lewis

I t's the things you don't expect that really drag you down into the darkness. More than a dark night of the soul, I had a dark season of the soul. In the midst of shifting life circumstances and shifting career objectives and shifting romantic relationships, I started to wonder what you could *really* trust, what was truly solid. For decades—my whole life—my faith had been the solid ground I stood on. It's what I was raised in. It was my normal. My reason for living. But now, after a series of events, I was starting to question what I believed in.

You know by now that I grew up in the church, and I was *all in.* I served. I evangelized. I was extreme. I edited video tapes to invite people to church, the whole nine yards. I felt God in my life. It was real to me. But it all started to crumble when the non-denominational Christian church I went to, Malibu Vineyard, went through multiple splits, and a few dark things happened that were extremely hard to process. Sure, the band Lifehouse was our youth group band (half the girls, me included, probably showed up because everyone had a crush on the lead singer—who could blame us?), but then I started to uncover all that had been going on behind the scenes.

I found out my youth pastor had molested a handful of the young men in our youth group. When the lies were uncovered, he fled the country back to South Africa without any apologies or goodbyes. We all felt duped, confused, brainwashed, and—honestly—like fools. One of the hardest parts of being manipulated and exploited is that you inexplicably and tragically feel like it's your fault.

Sure, there were signs. Small things. But despite the few things that made us question, we were all so enamored with his "spiritual gifts" and in awe of his "anointing" and how multiple people would be "slain in the Spirit" when he prayed for them. That's church language for when people put their hand on your head, and you fall down (or they push you down to make it look like God made you fall). The over-spiritualizing of everything "good" kept us from acknowledging or questioning things that seemed "off."

Naturally, finding this out about my church, my home—the place where I found myself, my happiness, and my identity—spun me into a tailspin of questions and no answers. What do you do when the place and the people in which you found safety and comfort do terrible things? I confidently put my whole heart into that community and was left with a whole lot of confusion.

After all this, and based on a myriad of other issues that followed, I decided to stick it out to see where the church would land. I ended up being the last one standing. I followed my senior pastor to the end, visiting him on his deathbed in his final days of fighting cancer. He was a major father figure to me, and I'm forever grateful for him.

But then the church was taken over by his son and his son's mentor, and that mentor started believing in polygamy and saying the Holy Spirit "gave him that revelation." That is when I drew the line and PEACED OUT. I was trying to find my feet underneath me, but it was like I was running on a floating log. Every mentor I looked up to had fallen, and I started feeling like my whole life had been a lie.

So I threw the baby out with the bathwater, and for the first time in my life, I wasn't sure if I even believed in God anymore. I felt like a tiny ant on this huge planet, lost in the midst of billions of other people, depressed and alone. I realized that for my whole life, I had fundamentally believed there was something special about me (and each one of us), that I was a unique individual created by God for a purpose. Now I was questioning that. I had always felt God was watching over me, but now that was gone, too.

I'd still periodically go to different churches because I was searching for that connection, comfort, and fulfillment I used to have. But when I went, it rarely sat well with me and all of my new conflicts and questions. It felt fake, "showy," and cookie-cutter-like, as though everything was stale and on repeat, no matter what church it was. I wasn't buying it. I'd seen the other side.

When my car broke down at a gas station (I drove my dad's cool, vintage, classic old hand-me-down, all-white Checker Marathon), I met a man who had taught philosophy at the Vatican. He was a walking encyclopedia. I started emailing him all of my existential questions and forwarding his answers to my other friends who were searching. I then decided to start a "Philosophy Night" at my apartment, during which he'd come with a white board and a stack of college philosophy books. I'd invite all of my ex-Christian friends as well as friends from every religion and walk of life. I'd buy us all wine and cheese, and we'd debate the night away. "Philosophy Night Thursdays" lasted two years.

So I started to explore other philosophies and religions—from atheism to Buddhism.

I loved what I had experienced about the Jewish religion and culture: the emphasis on family, Friday night Shabbat dinners, the commitment, the tradition, the order.

I dove in and got a job in a strict, fully kosher Orthodox Jewish restaurant. The men wore yarmulkes, and I'd serve everyone traditional Jewish prayer books. They'd wash their hands in the special station before they were allowed to talk.

It was all so fascinating and inspired something within me. Coming from all the chaos and emotionalism of my particular church, I was comforted by what felt like a firm foundation. I didn't necessarily want to convert per se; it was more that I was searching for wisdom and the reason for living wherever I could find it. I also explored different Christian traditions, from Catholicism to Methodism. At one point I even stayed with some Franciscan friars at their monastery in the Bronx. (There were multiple bullet holes in the room I stayed in, which was concerning, but . . .) The friars were the coolest guys I had ever met. They sold all of their belongings and shared the robes they wore every day. They walked around their communities helping, encouraging, and feeding the poor.

One night, as I was out with some of the friars doing their street ministry work, we met up with Brie Larson for dinner, since she was on location filming in New York. As we were walking home, one of the friars spontaneously started doing a freestyle spoken word rap beat battle on the street corner in his Franciscan robe, which naturally drew quite a crowd. Our jaws dropped. It was impressive.

While I was staying at the monastery, one night I joined about ten of the friars in one of their tiny rooms, enjoying beers and asking each one his life story. I laughed the hardest I had in a long time. The friars had a simple, humble, servant-hearted, peaceful reverence for God I had never experienced anywhere before. It was the complete opposite of the modern, non-denominational, rock concert-like church I grew up in, with its smoke machines and strobe lights.

Far beyond what was "false," beyond the brokenness I had uncovered in my church, I had finally found something authentic about the faith. It gave me fresh hope.

When I think back to that season of exploring different faith traditions, seeking to find my own way, I come back to some of the lyrics of this song called "Even Now" by United Pursuit's Will Reagan. The song is about wrestling with doubt, how fast we come up on life's sharp edges, and yet despite all of this: "Even now, here's my heart, God"—what bold words to offer in so uncertain a world.

I've listened to this song for years now, and it still touches me because it expresses the real struggle of faith in real life—that things don't always go as planned. Yet even in my greatest moments of doubting, I still can't seem to successfully and freely live without a connection to and reliance on God.

I had to learn to be OK with not knowing all of the answers. I had to learn to live in the tension of uncertainty and the unknown. I wasn't going to let a crisis of faith hold me back. I was going to move forward, not just regarding what I did or didn't believe about spirituality, but also in my purpose and career.

After my NBC show didn't get picked up, I got back on the bandwagon (as you do) and started auditioning for the next pilot season. Except this time, The Giving Keys was blowing up, and I was bombarded daily with fires I needed to help put out. I remember being in audition waiting rooms (or cattle calls as they call them) with the other actresses waiting to be called in. They were all looking at their sides (the portion of the script the casting directors want to see you perform); going over their choices, notes, and further memorizing the lines like I always also used to do; but now, I was sitting there, frantically answering emails and tending to all of The Giving Keys needs before my auditions. I walked into every audition that season frazzled and ill-prepared, which led to not even one callback, which led to not getting called for any auditions the following season.

After booking the season before with such a reputable cast and crew, it was a huge disappointment. Things were not going quite as I had planned.

Here I was, entering my thirties, no husband, no kids, and no career in the fields I was pursuing and had always dreamed of. I had thought by then I would be raising kids on tour buses and/or film sets. Instead, my life was requiring me to show up at an office, attend board meetings, answer nonstop emails, wear collared shirts in an attempt to be taken seriously, and manage dozens of disgruntled employees (not our missional hires who were transitioning out of homelessness; it was mostly the millennials). None of it was what I had originally hoped for or envisioned. I found myself struggling.

Although I loved what we were doing with The Giving Keys and the number of people it was helping, I was not enjoying my newfound role as CEO. With all of the pressing responsibilities of running a company, I barely had time to focus on the part of The Giving Keys that I first fell in love with—the actual mission. I would have preferred my role to be casting vision and creating unique ideas and movements to inspire the world, as well as encouraging and taking people experiencing homelessness out to meals, like I'd done in the beginning. I would have loved to be on the ground with the actual people the products were touching. My new businesswoman hit-the-numbers-and-be-the-boss-nine-to-five (more like 24/7) lot in life was turning out to be much more stressful than I could have ever imagined.

I realize this may sound foolish to you. You might be thinking, "Really, Caitlin? You started this incredible social enterprise business, you're solving real problems in the world, and you're disappointed?!" But while everyone else saw me as "successful," I felt like my heart, creativity, gifts, and passion were dwindling inside because I was trapped inside the four walls of an office and lost in never-ending charts and spreadsheets. I was numb.

By now you know the drill as well as I do: life doesn't turn out how you think it will. It doesn't mean it's negative or bad, but you might be disappointed and have to work through some grief, work through letting go. It's hard to reconcile a lost dream. It's natural to see it as a failure—a personal failure. But sitting where I am now, I'd argue that your life might actually be better because things didn't go as planned.

In fact, life going against your plan might even be the answer to prayer you didn't even know you needed.

I would have never been able to dream up The Giving Keys before it was time, before all the puzzle pieces landed. It evolved over time—that's how it goes. But none of that takes away from the reality that when life turns out different than you hoped, there is an internal battle to work through.

So I had to get real with myself and uncover what was really going on. How did I end up here? Why did I start The Giving Keys? What were my motives? I needed to get back to the core of why I had done everything.

When I made space for this wrestling, I realized that for my whole life, there were two prayers I'd always prayed:

"God, give me your heart for people. I want to feel what you feel for people."

"Open all the right doors that are meant for me, and close all the wrong doors that are not meant for me."

As I got to the root of my dissatisfaction with my life, it hit me. My prayers had been answered.

In my younger years, I always said the reason I wanted to make music and act was to have a platform to speak about topics I was passionate about, in order to ultimately help people and be a catalyst for positive change. I always had a heart for people who were hurting, probably partly because mine was hurting too. Although I thought it would look different, The Giving Keys was an exact answer to these prayers. Not only that, but I realized my prayers during my years of pursuing the entertainment industry had been answered. It's just that the answer was perhaps something bigger and better for me to put my hands to.

This was all my purpose unfolding.

I truly believe with every ounce of my being that The Giving Keys is an expression of God's heart for humanity. The Giving Keys was his answer to my prayer, something I never in a million years could have come up with on my own, a dream that would not have originated in me. It had to evolve and be uncovered in the right timing. So in this way, The Giving Keys isn't just helping others. It's helping me. It helped me believe in God again and see the world the way he sees it.

I believe our true purpose has a way of doing this. It has a way of enriching others and also enriching us. It has a way of bringing us back to ourselves and back to God. It has a way of helping us shape and reshape our vision.

Our purpose is so much more than the ego-driven pursuit of chasing our dreams. And it may not be as flashy as you once imagined it. "The dream" might not look like you expected, but you can bet it will be a powerful force of good for you and those around you.

For myself, I had to pivot my role and learn to delegate to those who are better suited for management, organization, and numbers. Sometimes it's not a perfect puzzle, with all the pieces fitting together just so (like when you sell thousands of necklaces as holiday gifts and a shipping company loses thousands of them and thousands of people want refunds and you have to become a customer service ninja). But you can trust your deep, inner knowledge that you're doing the work you're placed on this earth to do even as you learn to find your place within that work imperfectly.

I believe God gives second, third, fourth, and tenth chances to redeem the broken, homeless, and lost. To show love, dignity and hope to the hopeless and overlooked. I believe it's an extension of his heart that we're able to provide jobs for people who are transitioning out of homelessness. Not only that, but I believe his heart breaks for the everyday person who is hurting and needs that word on the key for encouragement.

The keys create this ripple effect because not only should you embrace the word for yourself, but you also have a heightened awareness to pay attention to others around you. It's like a compassion homework assignment. To see people who are hurting and pass your key on to spread even more hope, strength, and love. I once gave a COURAGE key to my old friend from college as she began the process of "freezing her eggs" since she was in her late thirties, single, and wanted to have viable eggs with which to conceive a child when the time was right. She said she had felt alone going through such a rigorous process without a partner, but holding on to that key was a reminder that she could be brave and get through it, and that she wasn't alone. A year later, she passed on her COURAGE key to a coworker who had just suffered a miscarriage. The keys have a magical way of finding kindred souls, like magnets.

I think the key was passed on to one or two more people, and then, years later, it actually made its way back to the friend I had originally given it to. An acquaintance had heard her mother had breast cancer and was going through chemo, and she gave it back to her when she needed some more courage for a different reason in a new season.

It's a beautiful thing, and I truly believe it's our collective purpose to speak life and encouragement to each other when we need it most.

Then a new prayer was added as my go-to: "God, grant me the serenity to accept the things I cannot change, the courage to change the things I can, and the wisdom to know the difference. I surrender. I surrender to my higher power." (the first part of this prayer is attributed to theologian Reinhold Niebuhr, though it became popular through AA and various other twelve-step programs.)

I not only had to continuously surrender my career path, health issues, and broken dreams, but I also had to surrender my relationships.

One particular boyfriend—we'll call him Josh—was a huge part of my twenties. We dated on and off over the course of seven years, and I truly thought we would end up together (we even went to premarital counseling and all). When we finally broke up, I was beyond heartbroken.

As if normal breakups weren't hard enough, he was a successful actor, so every time we broke up, I'd have to see his face on billboards, buildings, and buses. His face was even on my hotel room key once, and another time on my Coffee Bean cup holder. I grabbed my drink, was about to take a sip, saw his face come close to my lips, and then, in shock, spilled my scalding hot latte all over myself. I thought I'd never be able to get over him, to stop loving him. I thought I was doomed—that I'd never meet anyone else I was as "in love" with or impressed by. I thought I could never escape him because of his fame and his larger-than-life face, which would be marketed in my face for the rest of my life.

In hindsight, I think he was what I *wanted*, but he was in no way what I actually *needed*. It's easier to see clearly when you have space and time as your guide, but at the time, I was utterly blinded by love and completely distraught.

When I knew deep down our relationship was nearing the end, I wrote the song "Consolation Prize," and it made me realize I didn't want to keep living this way. Songwriting has always been therapeutic for me. Writing "Consolation Prize" made we realize I was trying to be "good enough" for him, but to no avail, as that was just an unhealthy narrative. I realized I was feeling like a consolation prize when I knew I deserved and craved more. I had a revelation while writing the song, realized my worth, and adjusted the song to end with these lyrics:

> *I could walk on water, heal the blind,*
> *still not enough to change your mind.*
> *But I'm strong enough, and waited long enough,*
> *but you're not man enough, so I've had enough.*
> *And if I settle now, you will be my consolation prize.*

I actually read him the words to the song, and that's the last time we broke up.

That's called GETTING YOUR MOJO BACK, ladies.

I kept writing songs. I played the LA circuits of Hotel Cafe and the like because it was therapeutic. I'm grateful for that heart-break experience because it caused—and almost forced—me to come back around to my love of encouraging girls and women (including myself) to love and treat ourselves with dignity and respect, and not repeatedly give ourselves away to men/boys who don't know our worth and value.

Through our love saga, I wrote the song "Save That Pillow." It's a letter to a girl who kept giving herself to a guy who sweet-talks her, manipulating her for his own pleasure or high, and leaves her feeling used and ashamed. The song is supposed to empower and remind us women of our precious significance and virtue. That we are worth waiting for. That we are worth being pursued with a reverence.

So get down to the bottom of why
you're giving yourself away,
And save that pillow for someone who
will love you the right way.

I had to play it for myself countless times in order to summon the self-control to resist allowing Josh back into my life just because I wanted to feel validated, wanted, and "loved" in the moment.

I wrote the song in the midst of deep pain, but this turned to meaningful joy later as I heard from women that they listened to the song on repeat just as I had, and it reminded them of their strength and incomparable worth.

From this and other songs I wrote during this season of my life, I got another record deal under Capitol Record's indie label, Deep Well Records, run by *Glee*'s executive music producer, Adam Anders. We put out an EP, including some more therapeutic songs I had written to help me process life and see clearly. Adam shot a music video for my single, "Just Another Day," about the darkness of growing up in LA and touching on human sex trafficking topics. The next thing I knew, I was about to start my next music tour.

Fast forward a bit to after my on-and-off relationship with Josh. I was about to turn thirty, and I was depressed. I was afraid I was running out of time. To find a husband. To get married. To have babies. I grew up praying for and writing letters to my future husband. They were so pure and innocent. I pictured that he was this fairy-tale handsome, hilarious, loving, sacrificial man, made just for me. I wanted someone to laugh with, to cry with, to build a family and enjoy life with. And here I was, weekend after weekend, going to other people's weddings, buying more bridesmaid dresses. Hosting another friend's bridal or baby shower. I'd hold back tears and secretly go cry in the bathroom. It sounds foolish now, as I wish I appreciated the freedom I had. (I'm writing this now as a tired, married mother of two with hardly a moment to myself). But the longing was real at the time.

For the first time in my life (and after many therapy sessions), I thought the only way to cope was to try anti-depressants. I tried a couple of different kinds, both of which made me feel extremely "off." I got nauseous and felt drugged and lethargic. I did not feel like myself. The meds made me feel worse, so I stopped and continued to try coping with life on life's terms.

As it turns out, I wasn't doomed after all. The story of how I met my husband, Colin, is comin' in hot.

I was always the third wheel to my best friend, Virginia, and her husband, Johnny. They always invited me to tag along, and I was grateful. Christmas rolled around, and I got decked out to go to Mosaic Church's Christmas Eve candlelight service. And yes, I was on the "Where's my husband prowl," so I wore stilettos and an ungodly amount of eye liner. When it was over, Johnny and

Virginia started talking to this guy named Colin and his family. I recognized Colin. I had met him once, years ago, through another mutual friend, but I hardly knew the guy. I walked over to join the conversation.

Colin lived in Nashville, but his brother, sister-in-law, and their kids lived here in LA. He was in town visiting for the holidays. While we all chatted, he shared how a girl had just broken his heart, and he was working through it. I had no shame, nothing to lose at that point, and told him that he was hot and had nothing to worry about.

As Johnny, Virginia, and I headed home, they said, "Wait, what about you and Colin together?! What if he's your husband?! You guys would be perfect."

Unbeknownst to me, Colin's brother was telling him the same thing. So Colin got my number, and the next day, he invited me to his birthday brunch. I was nervous because I knew everybody there was trying to set us up. It was only noon, and I definitely drank too much wine to calm my nerves. I nervously rambled on and on about Josh and how we went to premarital counseling together. Talking nonstop about your ex always makes a great impression on a first date, I know. Even after that, though, Colin invited me to his birthday dinner that night.

There was definitely chemistry, and I found myself wondering what was happening. I'm not one to make the first move, but after dinner, my mojo kicked in, and I offered to give him a birthday shoulder massage. Foxi Nova would have been proud. It wasn't long before he asked if I could drive him to LAX to catch his flight back to Nashville. I really liked him, so of course, I said yes. During the drive there, we stopped to get gas and snacks. That's when things got a little close in the Doritos aisle, and we kissed against the crunching bags. Now *that's* a man who really knows the way to my heart.

We kissed again at the airport. I couldn't believe what was

happening. Colin said he wanted to keep getting to know me and asked if he could pursue me from Nashville. Again, of course, I said yes.

As soon as he got on the plane, he called. He called again the next morning. And he proceeded to text me every morning after that with messages like, "Today is the day the Lord has made, I will rejoice and be glad." It was adorable. Ahh, early love. So much to learn about each other. We were enjoying the process, the mystery, the crush.

We started talking for hours every day. He flew back to Los Angeles to take me on an official date two weeks later. Then, for Valentine's Day, he flew me to Nashville. He greeted me at the airport as I came down the escalator, holding a huge, handmade heart-shaped sign that said, "Caitlin Crosby Will You Be My Valentine?" He also tried to draw angel cherubs, which looked like demons—bless his heart. But it was the thought that counted. He got me my own hotel room, and decorated it with confetti, chocolates, and flowers in a wooden vase engraved with our initials. He even booked me a massage. I felt like I was living in a movie.

This was such a contrast to what I had previously experienced living in "a man's world." And my Peace-o-Meter was at peace.

Every girl is worth being pursued like this. You are worth so much more than settling for someone who is "keeping his options open." You are worth so much more than settling for someone you have to chase, someone who "isn't sure" about you. Your value is far more precious than rubies. Hold out for someone who sees you and your worth clearly. You and your precious, one-of-a-kind heart are worth it.

Dating long-distance had its challenges, but it was still extremely romantic. We were committed to do what it took to continue getting to know each other, no matter the cost.

Colin worked at a restaurant and played in a local band with his best friends. He drove an old, rusted, green Ford Explorer he'd had since high school. It only had one door that worked, so we had to climb in and out through the one door that worked. I loved how normal he was. It was so refreshing compared to my last boyfriend, who bought his friends cars for their birthdays and had to wear makeup on set daily, pose on the red carpet, and kiss girls on-screen for a living. I loved that Colin was just a country boy. I loved visiting him at his sister's farm outside of Nashville.

And I loved how he helped me love my own flaws. I always envisioned getting another reconstructive surgery done before I got married (to get rid of the hard boob and scars), and as we had conversations about the future, this was something I talked about with Colin. But I continued to chicken out and push it out of my mind in a kind of denial. Colin was supportive and always told me he would love and support me whatever I wanted to do, and that he loved me just as I was.

I'd often fly to New York to work The Giving Keys trade shows or sell keys at a swanky Fifth Avenue Henri Bendel pop-up, and Colin often flew there to meet me. We told each other "I love you" for the first time after seeing the Broadway show *Once* in New York. We were both crying at all the same parts. It was as if that's what made us realize our hearts were deeply connected, that we were aligned.

Colin practically went broke pursuing me long-distance. I'm grateful he was willing to do what it took for us to be together. Everyone deserves someone who will fight for them like that.

We dated long-distance for eight months, until I finally told him I couldn't take it anymore. We needed to see what consistent, real life together would be like. So Colin left his band, which was heartbreaking for him (it still is), and moved across the country to

LA to be with me and find out if we'd actually "work" living in the same town. It was time to see if we should take the next steps.

We dated for a few more months until, to my surprise, the day before I left for my next music tour, Colin proposed in a hot air balloon. It was magical. And he was a smart man to put a ring on it before I left town for a month to explore a new state every day with a van full of guys.

The next morning, I was off. During that tour, I blew out my vocal cords. I also started to realize I didn't really thrive or enjoy performing in front of people. The nerves were really getting to me, and I started having an incredible amount of anxiety. I dreaded getting onstage. Nightly whiskey hot toddies became my companion, but I hated feeling like I needed a drink to get up onstage again and again. Over the course of the tour, I ended up developing serious nodules on my vocal cords.

I came back and showcased for my record label right before I was set to go on my next radio tour to promote my single. But Adam, the executive producer, was extremely concerned with the state of my voice. He cancelled the radio tour and had me start a regimen of vocal rest (no talking), speech therapy, a change of diet, and acid reflux medications. Nothing helped. Different people on my team encouraged me to try anti-anxiety medication because they thought it would help me get out of my head and perform better. I know they were worried about me, and I was embarrassed, but I did not take that particular piece of advice.

I did continue the speech therapy and other regimens, but my voice never recovered, so I never went on that radio tour to promote the single. My song had some life to it organically, and again, people told me they heard it on the radio or Sirius XM satellite radio, but we still didn't get the hit we were hoping for. While I was a bit deflated about all that, I was simultaneously consumed with my engagement to Colin, planning a wedding, and all the responsibilities of The Giving Keys that my life naturally took on a new direction—again.

I never said the surrender part was easy, because it's not.

Within a few months, Colin and I were married. It all felt very "meant to be." I was pleasantly surprised by how fast life had turned around. But of course, marriage doesn't always turn out to be the perfect "happy ending" we fantasize about. Often, our "happy endings" are journeys, not destinations.

As it goes, at the beginning of our relationship, we were on our best behavior. We looked for ways to treat and surprise each other. Like most couples, we had our "honeymoon phase." Then things started to get REAL. And *really* tough.

Our high was high, and our low was low. Our first year of marriage was hard, but year two was a disaster. We got to the point where we hated each other. Our work dynamics were challenging because, as The Giving Keys was taking off for me, Colin was still trying to find his vocation and career in LA. He was struggling, understandably so, as he had uprooted his life in Nashville for me. He had left a band he loved and his best friends for me. When he moved to LA, he needed work, so he started working at a restaurant and leading worship music at a few different churches.

Meanwhile, The Giving Keys was taking up all of my time, and my work-life balance started to get off-balance. I was working and traveling nonstop, and it started putting a strain on our relationship. We were living such drastically different day-to-day lives, it was hard to stay connected. At the time, I was learning how to scale a business with eighty employees. I was incredibly overwhelmed trying to figure out how to manage it all, and I came home exhausted with nothing left to give. It felt like we had nothing in common anymore.

Colin started to work with a life coach, one with whom I disagreed. Adding to all this, Colin's drinking started to become an issue. It was a huge topic of our fights. (Thankfully, he's now been sober for over three years, so there's a light at the end of the tunnel.) There were nights when I was trying to go to sleep because I had to wake up early for a work meeting, and he would not come inside and stop drinking. There was one night when I got out of bed in my robe and went out to the front yard to find him still drinking. I held up his full glass and said, "This is going to ruin our marriage!" I was enraged and about to throw the glass against the wall (real stable, Caitlin, I know), but I stopped myself mid-throw. The alcohol spilled all over me—my hair, face, and robe were drenched. I sobbed— begging and pleading for him to stop—but I have since learned that it is never wise to try to have a rational conversation with someone who is under the influence.

We started going to marriage counseling every week. And I'm not kidding when I say we both literally hated each other. We even said those horrifying words to each other. It makes me cringe thinking of how painful that second year of marriage was.

My heart was broken. We fought every single day. I was undone. I didn't know what to do with what was happening in my marriage.

Enter the prayer, "God, grant me the serenity to accept the things I cannot change." I have learned that I can't control anyone. I couldn't control Colin, make him stop drinking, or convince him to stop drinking. All I could do was take care of my slice of the pie. I had to take care of myself and get as healthy and whole as I possibly could, so that I could be the best version of myself in our relationship. *That* I could control. And that, I decided, was how I would fight for my marriage—not by trying to control my husband.

"God, grant me the serenity to accept the things I cannot change." I'd worked hard. Given it my all. That's when this prayer really hit home for me. I realized I needed to surrender, to leave it all in my Higher Power's hands. I needed to accept the way things were and let go of trying to change the things I could not possibly be expected to change.

I think this is a great question for all of us: What's getting in the way of your serenity? Is it worth it? If not, what actions can you take to reclaim your serenity? Those are decisions and changes you will never regret—not for a lifetime.

Surrender gets a bad rap, I think. Some people think surrendering your life to God means giving up your own free will or even just giving up altogether. Even I fell into that trap for a while, so when things didn't "work out" the way I thought they should, I questioned my faith. But what if surrendering to God's purpose in your life really just means you do everything you know how to do, leave it all on the field, and trust that the outcome will be as it was always meant to be? This is what I've come to. I did everything I could in both of my entertainment industry careers, and I eventually had to let the chips fall where they may. I couldn't keep trying to force something that was no longer meant for me.

Meanwhile, with The Giving Keys, it was just open door after open door. It was like heaven opened the floodgates and poured out yesses over and over. I couldn't ignore it. It was too obvious. Sometimes surrendering isn't just about surrendering to hardships but allowing yourself to surrender to the good things, too.

We got into the biggest stores in the world, like Nordstrom, Starbucks, and even the most popular store in Paris, France at the time, Collette. Starbucks' VP of marketing actually emailed into our website and shared that someone had given her a STRENGTH key when she was going through chemo. It meant so much to her that she wanted to see if we'd be interested in being a part of their flagship Roastery Starbucks in Seattle. The whole thing seemed too good to be true. It was one of those moments when I said to myself, *This must be spam.*

I ended up flying to Seattle, met with some of the Starbucks team, and showed them one of our videos, "On a Mission To Pay It Forward." By the end of the video, there wasn't a dry eye in the conference room. They said, "You should have warned us, so we could have gotten tissues!" They were blown away by what we were doing and even more in love with our mission and brand.

We started selling our keys at the one Starbucks location and got word they were selling out. So I wrote a long email pitch asking if they would be interested in selling our products in more of their stores. But while this email sat in my drafts folder, Starbucks actually wrote *us*, asking if we would be interested in making more exclusive products for them. For five thousand of their stores worldwide! Again, a huge open door of YES for The Giving Keys.

I believe my brain alone could never have come up with something as special as The Giving Keys, something that would leave the world's top executives in awe. I believe it had to be inspired by all the prayers and breadcrumbs leading up to its conception. In fact, *my* plan looked *completely* different.

I thought I was catching my big break . . . when the NBC show of my dreams got cancelled.

I thought I knew what I believed . . . when my church went haywire and sent me into a spiral of doubt and confusion.

I thought I had found love . . . then went through the hardest breakup of my life. And after that, even when I *did* find the love of my life, I ran smack into the reality that marriage is much harder than I ever expected.

So you can see how all my "foolproof" plans worked out.

If I could go back in time and give myself a word of advice, I would walk right up to that young woman churning in uncertainty, and whisper in her ear, *What if there's something better on the other side of surrender? What if you made the choice to open your hands, to stop gripping so tightly to what you hope for, and started receiving the unexpected gifts life has for you?*

Looking back, it's laughably clear to me that all my angst and fear was a direct result of clinging too closely to my own plans. It's also clear to me just what God wanted to press into my open hands: a scrappy, tarnished, perfectly imperfect key.

Perhaps this is a symbol for all of us. Our plans and dreams always look more polished when we're making and dreaming them than when life plays out. But in our imperfections, our scrappy passions, our mistakes, and our lessons learned, that's where we find new possibilities unlocked.

chapter six

MAKE YOURSELF PROUD

My mission, should I choose to accept it, is to
find peace with exactly who, and what, I am.
To take pride in my thoughts, my appearance,
my talents, my flaws and to stop this incessant
worrying that I can't be loved exactly as I am.

—Anaïs Nin

Growing up in and around the entertainment industry in Los Angeles (aka: having headshots of yourself taken starting at age two) definitely makes for some fabulous therapy topics. I've been to hundreds upon hundreds of auditions. I have tried everything I could to impress the casting directors and land the parts—changed my hair and makeup to fit what they were looking for, memorized lines, took countless expensive acting classes, and covered up thousands of pimples in the bathroom before casting calls.

Each time, I'd walk in with high hopes about a role that could not only pay my rent for the entire next year, but could also change the trajectory of my life. I had high highs and crash-and-burn lows.

The overpowering nerves. Fumbling through lines. Fighting to blow away the casting directors, only to be met with a cold "Thank you," which I followed with a shameful walk out the door and a good cry in my car.

Despite all of it, like many others in this Hollywood hamster wheel, I kept coming back for more.

Getting a callback was thrilling. A callback is when they want to see you again and bring you back to audition for the producers, writers, and director—kinda like being asked out on a second date after a first date goes really well. But no high compared to the feeling I got when the phone rang and it was my agent calling to say, *You booked the role.* It was almost like a drug.

Because my parents were in the industry, and I saw how the world valued their successful actor clients, my motives were a bit convoluted. I think, deep down, I just wanted my parents to be impressed. I wanted so badly to feel valuable and worthy in their eyes. I wanted them to be proud of me.

My mother grew up just outside Washington DC in Silver Spring, Maryland. On a dare and a bet with a friend at the University of Maryland, she entered the Miss Maryland contest. To her shock—and a bit of dismay—she won. She was much more a hippie than a beauty queen. But her career took off. From there, she ended up going to New York, where she modeled for several years.

She called herself "the reluctant model" because it all seemed so superficial to her. She also developed a successful commercial career, and made over seventy-five commercials, including campaigns with legends like George Burns and Don Adams. While running in LA entertainment industry circles, she met my father, and they instantly hit it off.

My mother eventually got into TV as well, and she was cast to play the first female CHiP officer in a TV movie pilot spin-off of the TV series, *CHiPs*. And yes, she "had to do" kissing scenes with Eric Estrada. All my friends' moms were jealous, and my husband even said he used to have a crush on her. Although it sounds glamorous—acting, riding a Kawasaki 2000 motorcycle, getting paid to kiss big stars on-screen—she wasn't enjoying all that came along with being on that side of the camera. She later became a talent agent for kids and teens.

My mom also worked hard to raise me. She was a single mother for almost a decade. You've already heard about all she did to try to help with my health issues, but she also fostered in me a heart for people. My mother taught me, by example through word and deed, to have empathy for people—no matter who they were.

My mom's grandpa happened to be someone who experienced homelessness. He was an alcoholic who could not get his addiction taken care of. She remembers taking him food and clothes every week as a little girl. Her family attempted to help him get back in his apartment, but sadly, he couldn't beat his addiction and kept reverting back to living on the streets. This gave my mother a tremendous amount of compassion for people who are suffering or less fortunate.

The irony that my career and life's work has led me to people who are transitioning out of homelessness has not been lost on my mother. She used to take me to downtown LA to bring food and clothes to people out on the street. She taught me that sometimes people need help. Sometimes people need a second chance, and perhaps no one else will give it to them. She taught me to fight for the underdog, and that has always been a huge driver for me. She ingrained it in my soul.

So much so, in fact, that even in junior high and high school, I would break up fights. When big, tough guys twice my size got into fistfights, I would run into the center and physically break it up. I always stood up for the guy getting beaten up.

After the fight was broken up, I'd yell at the bully, then try to soothe both parties and help them talk through their issues, to see each other's sides and make up. It was just a natural response. It came from how my mom raised me—that I should always stand up for the underdog.

If my mom gave me her compassion and creative gene, my dad gave me his "don't mess with me," hard-worker DNA.

My dad was born in Liverpool, England and raised just a few blocks from where the Beatles made The Cavern Club famous on Mathew Street. His family moved to Los Angeles in the mid-1950s, and he graduated from Hollywood High School.

At a young age, he was hired at CBS Television City and primarily served as the page to old-school legends like Carol Burnett. Upon completing college, he was offered a position as an assistant to CBS's vice president of casting, who oversaw CBS classics like the original *Hawaii Five-O*, *The Wild Wild West*, and *Gilligan's Island*.

In the late '60s, a major European agent offered my dad his first big agent job in Beverly Hills. Mr. Frings represented the biggest star in Hollywood at the time—Audrey Hepburn. It was a once-in-a-lifetime opportunity. (Side note: my first AOL screen name was AudreyActCC. You can tell a lot about a person from their first AOL screen name. I grew up with posters of Audrey Hepburn all over my bedroom.)

The boutique agency my dad worked with also represented legends like Sophia Loren and Brigitte Bardot. During this time, my dad was introduced to The Doors' Jim Morrison. Jim expressed interest in writing and acting, and my dad became his agent in those fields. They worked together until Jim's untimely death in Paris in 1971.

In the early '70s, my dad worked as a theatrical agent at one of the top agencies in Hollywood to this day, ICM. He later opened

John Crosby & Associates in the mid-70s to specialize in new, young talent. He helped discover and start the careers of stars like Jamie Lee Curtis and Fran Drescher. He spotted Rene Russo at a Rolling Stones concert when Rene was seventeen years old. He guided her through a career at Ford Models, where she became one of the first supermodels, then managed her during her years as a movie star. Rene has been referred to as the most beautiful woman in the world. My dad was introduced to The Rolling Stones' Mick Jagger during that time as well. Mick, like Jim Morrison, was exploring the possibility of trying his hand at acting and producing movies. My dad respected Mick and thought he was brilliant. He represented him for several years.

All this success helping and working with big names in the entertainment industry led to ABC offering my dad the vice president of casting position for ABC Television. He oversaw all of the casting of ABC from 1982–1988. While there, he initiated the ABC Talent Development program, where new talents such as George Clooney, Robin Wright, Arsenio Hall, and Sinbad were on annual contracts with the goal of assisting them towards an ABC series at the very beginning of their careers.

Since developing new talent was always my dad's passion, he decided to open JCM (John Crosby Management) in the late '80s. He went on to develop the film career of Rene Russo in such major films as *The Thomas Crown Affair, Tin Cup, In the Line of Fire, Get Shorty,* the *Lethal Weapon* franchise, and the recent films *Thor* and *The Avengers.* He's had a forty-year working relationship with Rene Russo, only to be matched by his forty years of representing the late great English actor and Oscar nominee John Hurt.

And of course, as I already mentioned, my dad also represented Charlize Theron. He started with Charlize when she was nineteen years old and helped in the early development of her career throughout her massive rise to the top. He discovered Shia LaBeouf when he was twelve and has represented him for the past twenty years. Dad believes Shia is possibly the greatest actor of his generation.

So you see, my parents have both had quite a ride during their careers, and this is the family I grew up in. The norm. As the only child of my parents, I was surrounded by critically acclaimed celebrities, press, premier parties, fame, and notoriety. No wonder I wanted so badly to work in the entertainment industry. I remember watching some of the most iconic scenes from movies being filmed as I sat and watched from the sidelines with stars in my eyes (and, of course, stealing snacks from the craft service tables). I remember going with my dad to Charlize's famous rockstar boyfriend's birthday parties and watching "young Hollywood" carrying on and having a good ol' time. Once, someone came up to me, smoking, and said, "Do as I say, not as I do."

It was at these parties that I learned power and privilege are not the ingredients for a life of fulfillment and peace. But I still craved it. I think we all want to make our parents proud. I know they were and are proud of me, but at that age, it was all tangled up from my point of view.

A study in *Psychology Today* interviewed seventy-five high-performing, "successful" women, and 100 percent still saw success through the lens of their fathers.[*] So it makes sense that it's difficult to rise above those perceived expectations and create your own path of success, which may look different from what you grew up around.

Years later, my father told me he had found a loose journal entry of mine in which I wrote about being insecure because of

---

[*] Peggy Drexler, PhD, "Daughters and Dad's Approval," *Psychology Today* (blog), June 27, 2011, https://www.psychologytoday.com/us/blog/our-gender-ourselves/201106/daughters-and-dads-approval.

all of my dad's female clients, and from that day on, he stopped managing ingenues and leading ladies. I felt a mixture of guilt and gratitude. I have now come to accept that as love.

In high school, I remember getting the call that I had booked my favorite TV show, *7th Heaven* (I know there are some die-hard *7th Heaven* fans out there). When my mom told me, I dramatically threw myself into the back seat of her car and starting kicking and screaming, elated. That was one of the highest highs I had ever felt. Probably not very healthy in retrospect, but it was real. Ironically my "good Christian girl" self was cast as the "mean girl" in *7th Heaven*. But I didn't even care. I was *on* my favorite TV show.

That audition turned out to be a good one, but man, do I have some fail stories. My number-one favorite fail was when I auditioned for the *Buffy the Vampire Slayer* spin-off called *Angel*. The scene started off with the character I was auditioning for crying and screaming because she was being chased by some sort of a demonic dog-type creature.

I was always terrified of having to cry in an audition because it was so hard for me to conjure the tears in the midst of all those nerves. The casting director knew my father, which made me extra nervous. I didn't want to embarrass my dad, so I came overly prepared. I thought to myself, "OK, what would make me cry?" "Onions!" Before the audition, I cut one in half and put it in a plastic bag in my purse, along with a knife to get a fresh cut right before I walked in. To really help myself out, I also sat in my car before the audition and listened to Bette Midler's song "Wind Beneath My Wings" on repeat. That song always made me cry. I was desperate.

I rubbed the onion juice on my fingers and was planning on rubbing it near my eyes right when I walked in the audition room and began the scene. This was going to work perfectly. But. (You knew there was a "but" coming in this story, right?) I accidentally got the onion juice *in* my eye. So instead of nice steady tears like I was going for, I just looked like I was in a lot of awkward pain. Probably because I *was*. It was a disaster. A cringe-worthy performance.

Then, to top it all off, when I finished the scene, the casting director looked at me and said, "I'll tell your father you're pretty." Uh, thanks? I walked out and THEN started crying (fifteen minutes too late). I was mortified.

I've come to this conclusion: If you live your life trying to impress other people, it will be a lifelong journey of dissatisfaction. Why? Because making everyone happy is an impossible task. Not to mention, it comes at great personal expense.

If we spend our lives striving to impress, please, and earn the love of parents, partners, peers, employees, and social media gods, we'll only be disappointed. It's exhausting just thinking about it. What an excruciating and miserable life that would be. I've spent too many days doing just that. Seeking approval and purpose by pleasing others. Any other Enneagram 2s out there? You feel me.

At the end of the day, and more importantly, at the end of our lives, I think we will all feel like we've finished well if we simply feel proud of ourselves. We all have our own stories, our own experiences. Only you know the depth of what you've gone through, and I'm here to tell you that you must give yourself grace on your journey. There's more than enough comparison and worry about being good enough out there to last a lifetime. How liberating would it feel to be able to move through your life in confidence and truly be proud of yourself? Really proud of yourself?

The big question is, *How?*

The best way I know how to do that is to make a trade. An upgrade, if you will. Let's trade all the energy we would have spent on impressing other people—whose impressions, by the way, we can never control—for energy we can spend on making choices we *can* control and be proud of.

I know that letting go of what other people think of you is a learned skill, and like many, I had to learn it the hard way.

Since my dad was managing Charlize during my most formative years as a teenager, that shaped who I am today. It was always a mixture of excitement—to be able to go to all of her premieres and parties, to see behind the scenes of her day-to-day life and rise to stardom—and deep insecurity. I felt I was always in her shadow, never measuring up to her greatness.

Everyone was so enamored by her. She was like the ultimate cool, perfect big sister. But it was challenging for me to see her larger-than-life on billboards and magazine covers, not to mention winning an Oscar for best actress, because I constantly compared myself to her. She was killing it, and I was still going to auditions for Taco Bell commercials. (Although all the fast food commercials I did paid my rent for a decade, so I'm grateful. And yes, I took hundreds of bites of hundreds of chalupas and spit into a bucket after each take. Glamorous.)

Though I was booking more jobs than most of my friends and peers who were also pursuing acting, it paled in comparison to Charlize's success. So I never really felt proud of myself. Everything I did felt lame compared to her accomplishments. The entire world raved about her. See how insidious comparison can be? It not only steals our joy, it steals our purpose. As long as I was looking at Charlize, I couldn't see the clear signs right in front of me, showing the way to who I was all along.

Each time I'd see Charlize on another billboard, getting bigger and bigger, I felt smaller and smaller. Even years later, after we've lost touch, I still sometimes get a twinge of PTSD when I see her face on billboards. This says nothing about Charlize, by the way, as she is truly a wonderful person. This is just what happens when we let comparison take control. It takes over our minds and hearts, and no matter what we do, we won't feel like we are good enough. It wouldn't have mattered if I thought I was better than Charlize; I would have found someone else to compare myself to. As long as comparison rules in your heart, you'll have to constantly fight feeling less-than. Comparison is a slow-working poison.

Theodore Roosevelt is credited with having said, "Comparison is the thief of joy." This quote is one of my all-time favorites. It reminds me that comparing your work, your life, or whatever else you have with what someone else has will only serve to make you unhappy. You're setting yourself up for loss. There will always be someone who is more this or that. This rings so true for me. The more I compare myself to others, the more uneasy I become. I realize some of this is natural and how we are programmed, so it's imperative that we become intentional about stopping those thoughts, or, as I like to say, "holding our thoughts captive" (something I pulled from old church youth group days, paraphrasing Paul's words in 2 Corinthians) We must intentionally train our minds to celebrate our uniquenesses and meditate on things that are healthy and life-giving (see Philippians 4:8).

I think this is why social media can be so harmful and toxic. It can be a dangerous place to get caught up in comparison. We have to be aware and guard ourselves from getting sucked into the vortex. We have to train our minds to be stronger than our habits and emotions and feed our eyes and hearts with truth about our unique identity and purpose in life.

There will never be another you! How sad would it be if your "you-ness" was wasted? What if you didn't enjoy the fact that you're the only you who will ever be here?

To get scientific, the odds of you being born are one in four hundred *trillion*. You are a miracle. Dr. Ali Binazir illustrates the extremely unlikely chain of events that would have to occur in order for you to be born: "Imagine there was one life preserver thrown somewhere in some ocean and there is exactly one turtle in all of these oceans, swimming underwater somewhere. The probability that you came about and exist today is the same as that turtle sticking its head out of the water—in the middle of that life preserver. On one try."*

Your one-of-a-kind birth mother somehow met your one-of-a-kind birth father, and together they made something unprecedented in all of human history: you. One-of-a-kind you. Your one-of-a-kind fingerprints, your one-of-a-kind soul, your one-of-a-kind body and gifts and brilliance. What if we wasted time wishing something that was literally scientifically impossible: to be like someone else? No. You, my dear, just as you are, are a miracle. You can never be copied or duplicated. Your story is unlike any other. So let's make it a good one.

I think some people were raised, conditioned, or born to have self-confidence. I think many of us who grew up in a faith culture that teaches us the importance of being "humble" can sometimes end up learning a different, negative trait instead—extreme lack of self-confidence—which can be disguised as humility. For those of us who haven't found it easy or natural to love or believe in ourselves, we need to work at it. I believe it's a discipline we must put

---

* Dina Spector, "The Odds of You Being Alive Are Incredibly Small," *Business Insider*, June 11, 2012, https://www.businessinsider.com/infographic-the-odds-of-being-alive-2012-6.

into practice and cultivate. I think we need to train our minds to silence the lies. We need to train our minds to say, "No," and stop the mental spiral when we start to let other people's paths or opinions steer us. How do we learn to stay in our own lanes? How do we learn to own our own stories and be proud of them?

Studies have shown that gratitude can help retrain our brains with positive beliefs about our lives and ourselves. According to UCLA's Mindfulness Awareness Research Center, regularly expressing gratitude literally changes the molecular structure of the brain, serving almost like vitamins for our gray matter, making us healthier and happier. Gratitude lights up parts of the brain's reward pathways. In short, just like Prozac, gratitude can boost neurotransmitter serotonin and activate the brain stem to produce dopamine, the feel-good hormone.

To take gratitude to the next level, writing and speaking daily affirmations about ourselves can also aid us in feeling proud of ourselves.

As one researcher puts it, "Affirmation takes advantage of our reward circuits, which can be quite powerful."[*] Studies show that affirmations can reduce the experience of pain in the brain, strengthen our sense of resilience, and increase our ability to manage stress. Our brains are muscles, which means we have to exercise them to change the negative pathways that have been ingrained over time. I use affirmations regularly. Here are a few examples you can use, too:

I am strong.
I am capable.

---

[*] "How Affirmations Help Develop Self-belief in Children," Ripple Kindness Project (website), Aug. 10, 2015, https://ripplekindness.org/why-affirmations-are-important-for-children/.

I am lovely.

I am worthy of love.

I deserve to enjoy my life.

I am creative.

I am beautiful inside and out.

I am brave.

I am intelligent.

I am special.

Copy mine or write your own to reflect what you need to believe about yourself. We are brainwashed all day long by the media and old narratives and scars from our experiences, so we must fight for our mental health and positive thinking. We literally have to reprogram ourselves and speak positive, healthy truths into our lives.

I used to go to a therapist named Dr. Jackie Jayne Brandt, who has since passed away. She taught cognitive behavioral therapy (CBT), which is a basic form of therapy that teaches you to change your thought patterns so that you can change the way you feel about yourself. I remember Dr. Brandt saying you can look at your mind like a record player. We have these scars, like dents in the record, that get caught when we're triggered. The grooves get deeper and deeper when we hear something that confirms a negative belief about ourselves. When we are in a negative cycle, sadly, we spend our days looking for confirmation of our negative beliefs. We then say to ourselves, "See? They said that, or they think that, or that happened, so that confirms that I really am this way!"

The "deepest groove" in my record was not feeling feminine or sexy enough. So you can see why Charlize on a billboard, and execs in a rehearsal screaming, "Be sexy, Caitlin!" and french fries being swatted out of my hand, and the deformity of my breasts were all trigger points for me feeling less-than. I was convinced that everyone thought that, everyone saw it as the same "glaring" problem I did. So whenever someone reacted a certain way, I'd assume the worst and make my negative record-player indention even deeper.

Dr. Brandt taught me that I can't necessarily just pray away those negative tapes. Instead, I had to create new, deeper grooves in my record that were the exact opposite of my negative beliefs so my record player wouldn't always get caught on the negative grooves. She gave me a homework assignment and helped me create a one-sentence affirmation that stated the exact opposite of how I felt. She said it needed to be a strong statement, an extreme, over-the-top contrast to my negative beliefs, in order to work.

My affirmation to reprogram myself was, "I am THE sexiest and most sensual woman I have ever seen in my entire life." I wrote this out multiple times a day and even put it on Post-it notes in my car and on my bathroom mirrors. On top of this, Dr. Brandt told me I'd have to start by acting this way in my private life. She asked me, "How would 'the most sexy and sensual woman in the world' drive her car? How would she order coffee from the barista at Coffee Bean?"

I remember driving and singing along to Lenny Kravitz's song, "American Woman," and getting very into it, bobbing my head back and forth to swing my hair, I started to actually feel a tinge of confidence and freedom in my femininity. It was one of the most joyful feelings I had ever felt.

A therapist I love, Ann Warford, said, "Crossing the threshold from comparison to selfhood is a short journey if you are willing to awaken and step outside the prison cell."

We all teach best what we most need to learn.

Back in the days of Foxi Nova, we got to sit down to dinner with the one and only Mariah Carey. This goes down as one of my all-time most special memories. Every girl my age grew up listening to and idolizing Mariah, so to sit across from her and share a meal was incredible. But what was even more special was that she opened up to me about her life. I happened to have Mary Mary's gospel CD in my purse. I don't remember how it came up, but when Mariah saw it, she perked up.

She said that CD had gotten her through some really hard times. I obviously won't go into what she said, but I'm forever grateful to Mariah for being vulnerable that night. It was a stake-in-the-ground moment for me. A reminder of a woman's strength. A reminder to stand up for myself. To tread through the mud and take courage. To be bold in the face of people trying to forcefully influence who I am and what I'm about.

At the end of the day, I always have my voice.

After that dinner with Mariah, when our team wanted us to sing songs that "pushed the envelope" in an attempt to get that "hit" I started feeling better and better about saying no. One of my favorite sayings from Glennon Doyle is, "The most revolutionary thing a woman can do is not explain herself."* I wish I'd had that quote back then. Besides overtly sexual songs and songs about fake IDs, the team pushed even further, wanting us to sing a song about having an affair with a married man. One of the lines in the song went, "I see that wedding ring on your finger but I just don't care." C'mon, people. We were teenagers, for crying out loud. Besides, the world deserves better. So I told them so.

---

* Glennon Doyle, quoted in Heidi Stevens, "'Love Warrior's' Glennon Doyle Melton opens up about new love, Abby Wambach," *Chicago Tribune*, Nov. 14, 2016, https://www .chicagotribune.com/columns/heidi-stevens/ct-glennon-doyle-melton-abby-wambach -balancing-1114–20161114-column.html.

I told them there was no way I'd sing those lines. They tried to pressure us. They threatened to not pay our monthly retainer and rent. They were basically paying us to be their "products" and to do everything they said. But I still put my foot down. Thankfully, it worked. They eventually let it go and moved on to the next song.

Speaking out against the grain and standing up for yourself stretches and tests you. But what you gain by doing so is priceless. You preserve your dignity. And you will never regret preserving your dignity.

We all have to draw a line somewhere, and we all have choices. Some things you know you need to stand up for can feel small, but they will add up to integrity. People may pressure you and try to make you feel small, but at the end of the day, you answer to yourself and God, and that's it. It takes courage, but deep down, you know what you need to do. Listen to that voice.

One day, we were in the studio, recording a song I wrote with Babyface about faith (yes, they finally liked one of my Goody Two-shoes songs). The tapes were rolling, and Christine was singing her verse. I could tell she was really struggling that day to nail her part. She tried take after take, and I could tell she was holding back tears. So I asked Babyface if I could go in and give her a private little pep talk. He said sure.

I went into the recording booth, which was behind soundproof doors, and took her over to the corner of the room so no one could see or hear us. I told her how talented and capable she is and asked if she wanted me to pray with her before she went back to give her an extra boost. She said yes, and then she opened up her hands to receive. I placed my hands on her and prayed. I prayed that as she sang those lyrics about fighting for your faith, she would be free to sing with conviction, power, authenticity, freedom, and complete abandonment.

I 100 percent thought this was all done in private since we were in a soundproof room and hidden in the corner. But when she went back into the recording booth, and I came out into the room where Babyface was, his jaw was dropped. He said, "I'm not gonna mess with you anymore."

He brought me into his private room, which had security monitors showing every square inch of the studio. He showed me how he had seen on video what we were doing, turned up the microphone, and heard the prayer. He told me that after hearing my prayer, he was going to take me more seriously since he now knew I was "not playing around." Though I had no intention at the time of anyone seeing or hearing that special time with Christine, the incident empowered me to believe in myself a bit more. To not be so hesitant to speak up and share my truth. To believe in my ability to be a force for good and justice, no matter where I found myself. To be proud of myself.

I hope you'll find a way to be proud of yourself, too.

Instead of beating yourself up for all the balls you're dropping, why not choose to be proud that you've somehow attracted so many wonderful things in your life to juggle? And of course, with all of those things piled up, it's only natural that a few of them will fall. You don't have seventeen hands. It's simple math, people.

Give yourself grace to be more human. Be proud of yourself every time you're tempted to say yes, but then you say no. Be proud of your boundaries, a sign that you're trading people-pleasing for respecting yourself.

Be proud of yourself every time you prioritize self-care.

Be proud of yourself that you made it through that lay-off, that divorce, that death, that grief.

Be proud of yourself when you clean out your fridge and cook a healthy meal.

Be proud of yourself every time you push the pause button and take deep breaths.

Instead of picking apart all the little things you wish you'd done differently, allow yourself to fall in love with all the little things you *do* and all the little things you have to offer this world. Go on, I dare you, make yourself proud. I am quite confident you'll begin to feel the difference.

chapter seven

GIRL BOSS IN THE ER

If the highest aim of a captain were to preserve
his ship, he would keep it in port forever.

—Thomas Aquinas

"Be careful what you wish for" could also be the title of this
chapter. I don't mean for that to sound ominous. I just mean to
say that sometimes, the blessings we pray into our lives are so much
bigger than us, they nearly swallow us alive.

When I first started The Giving Keys, nothing sounded more
wonderful and exciting than the very opportunities that were now
in front of us: Nordstrom. Starbucks. Massive worldwide orders we
were having to stretch ourselves to fulfill. It seemed like we could
hardly keep up with the snowballing success of the company. What
more could you ask for when you're running a giveback movement
and company that's fighting to provide jobs for those transitioning
out of homelessness? The better the company does, the more sales
we have, and the more people we can help get off the streets.

And while, of course, these are the kinds of things you *wish* for when you begin, I'm not sure we always know what we're asking. What you don't realize before you step into your purpose is how it is sometimes bound to take you into situations that are so far over your head, you may not have the wisdom and experience to know what to do with them. You're presented with problems so far beyond your pay grade that you don't have the tools to solve them. And everyone is looking to you for the answers.

People often say, "Wow, you're so lucky that you get to have your own company, can be your own boss, and make your own schedule and not have to answer to anyone." If only it were that simple and painless. At times, the stress and weight feel unbearable, especially because I never had a dream to become "the boss." It was never my goal. Remember, the *only* way I got here was by surrendering what I thought my life plans should be.

When I started The Giving Keys, it was my "side passion project." I loved the freedom to be creative and just make whatever words or jewelry or campaign or post I felt inspired to make. I let people pay whatever they wanted for them. And honestly, I gave away most of the jewelry to people who needed the words on it. People who were experiencing homelessness, girls who attended my shows, celebrities. Everyone needed those words, so I shared them. I didn't have to manage anyone in any organized way. I didn't have to review any spreadsheets, crunch numbers, or frantically try to meet our budget to be able to pay employees, vendors, or office rent. There were no contracts. There was no HR. There were no structured meetings. There weren't hundreds of emails a day. There was no stress. There was freedom to create and innovate without restrictions, rules, or limits. It was scrappy. Guerrilla-style. My favorite style.

Somewhere along the way, it got so big that I had to start delegating to people who were trained professionals, and I lost control of my ideas, voice, and heart. It all started to get buried by so many opinions and by so many cooks in the kitchen. There had to be plans, calendars, and deadlines implemented in order to productively scale and run the business in an organized fashion. Often, when I had opinions, they didn't fit into the business's box, or they weren't HR compliant. In hindsight, I wish I had stood up for what I felt was best in certain circumstances, but it was like walking a tightrope because when I would push my ideas, employees would often complain I wasn't letting them do their jobs. They wanted to feel like their boss trusted them (rightly so). It was hard to find the balance, so instead, I would often shut down, which caused resentment to simmer because I felt like I didn't have a voice in my own company anymore. This was my baby. It was my everything, and I didn't know where I fit anymore.

Being a boss didn't come naturally to me, to be honest. I had a lot of new skills to learn, and I was plagued with impostor syndrome, which showed up in constant self-doubt and second-guessing my decisions. Being a boss also sometimes means you should make the "best business decision" by firing someone, and I'd always choose not wanting to negatively impact their lives or hurt their feelings over the needs of the business. I still struggle with that today.

So I've had to research and hone that skill (thank you, podcasts, TEDx talks, and business authors). I worked with a leadership coach, Jason Jaggard, and shared with him how worked up I would get when the team didn't carry out my requests. He said something to the effect of, "Would you rather get every single thing done the way you want it to be done, or would you rather be happy?" That stung in the best way and has stuck with me since. Thankfully, after a lot of learning and trial and error, I finally feel like I've got my voice back. I've found a balance between asking for what I want; fighting for things I know need to happen; and knowing when to back down, let go of control, and be a team player. But I still have a lot to learn.

People don't see all the behind-the-scenes pressures, the financial debt and personal guarantee loans from banks that could wipe out my family's home and life savings if The Giving Keys isn't able to perform and keep up. People have come to my house to serve me papers in front of my family (aka, "We are suing you and taking you to court" papers). No one sees the sleepless nights and actual nightmares that all came with owning and running a company, the up-at-two-a.m. frantic writing of emails about a printing company trying to sue us for $50,000 while simultaneously clicking over one tab to add names to my baby shower list. Never quite present in the nesting mindset of enjoying so many of life's blessings while still always putting out fires.

I was a few days past my due date with baby number two, Love, and I was at the hospital waiting to see if we were going to induce. I was hooked up to a monitor for a stress test on her heart rate, having actual contractions, and simultaneously fielding frantic messages from my CFO that we needed to get another loan to make it through the month. So I needed to get on a call with the financial loan company to sign off—IN THE MIDDLE OF A CONTRACTION.

It's difficult to find out employees are disappointed with me when I'm not in the office as much as they would like, and they assume I'm only working when they see me there. I know they will never see how much I sacrifice for the mission, but I struggled with wanting to fix it and prove to them how much I did. If only they saw me writing work emails from inside a crib while my child was longing for me to be present with him. Leaving Brave with a nanny so I could work literally broke my heart every single day. And some employees still felt like I wasn't doing enough. I felt like I was failing my children and family as well as The Giving Keys. It felt like a lose-lose.

My husband once told me, "The Giving Keys is eating you alive," and maybe that was the first time I noticed it—although it was still a long time before I listened. I didn't stop to listen until my body literally began to fall apart.

I've since learned to embrace the notion that it's none of my business what other people think of me. It's another opportunity to grow and put that unhealthy side of the Enneagram 2 to bed.

One of our most endearing employees was a man named Leon. He had the kindest eyes and the brightest smile. It could light up a room. We employed him through one of our nonprofit partners, since he was in the process of trying to transition out of homelessness. He was very eager to learn, grow, and succeed at changing the trajectory of his life. He had been to prison, but he was a sweet, lovable, teddy-bear kind of guy. He became our shining star. He was an example to every new employee. He wore collared shirts every day and got many promotions.

His dream was to start his own social enterprise selling scarves to benefit sickle cell anemia research and foundations—a disease he wanted to fight based on its effect on his own life. Our team supported him in trying to help make his goals come true. We helped him with product designs, how to source the materials, and we gave him website and graphic design support. It was all free help, mainly after hours but sometimes even during The Giving Keys work hours (when he was getting paid to work for us).

After Leon had worked for us for quite some time, we agreed to hire his long-time fiancée. We all loved and trusted her, too. Unfortunately, after a while, she wasn't getting along with some of our other production employees. This caused Leon to shift his behavior at work. Gone was the sweet teddy-bear-like presence.

He started to ask for more raises, and when he was met with reasons why leadership didn't think it was an appropriate time to give him a raise, he grew angry. Something was happening, and we couldn't quite put our fingers on what the problem was, but Leon was no longer the person we'd hired.

One day, he came to work unusually early and brought a backpack with him, which he'd never done before. Our production manager noticed him walking around the office, particularly checking to see if our company president, Brit had arrived. The production manager grew concerned that something was off. She had a conversation with him in the alleyway to try to understand what was going on. She asked Leon if he was OK, and he went off about how upset he was with "what had been going on" and said that he "didn't like what was going on." Then he said he didn't feel well and needed to leave.

Even though Leon's behavior was erratic and a little alarming, the production manager bravely leaned into the conversation, trying to be supportive and understand what was upsetting him so much. After several more questions, he proceeded to tell her he'd brought a gun to work and was planning to use it. This was obviously incredibly disturbing but explained the backpack and the unusual behavior. The production manager had never been faced with something like this before. She spoke calmly with Leon, her mind now turned towards how to de-escalate the situation and get him safely off the premises. Through the de-escalation process, they agreed that he should leave, so he did, taking his backpack with him. The production manager, shaken up quite a bit, immediately informed HR, who in turn contacted Brit to come up with a plan. The immediate action was to get everyone out of the office and working from home in case Leon came back to the office. An all-staff meeting was called. Everyone was told that there was a safety concern and that we would be closing the office for the day. The next step was to notify the police.

Brit then called me and filled me in. The police wanted us to meet them in an obscure open area. They directed us to meet them in the middle of an Office Depot store in downtown LA (this scene felt VERY *CSI*). Brit and I stood in the middle of the store and explained what happened. We were all extremely shaken up as the reality of the situation was hitting us—Leon could have ended people's lives that very morning at our office. There was such a mix of emotions flooding my body. Fear for my life and the lives of my team members. Anger that someone we'd invested so much in would ever dare to do such a thing. Gratitude that no one had actually been hurt.

Since we couldn't afford to move our entire business to a new location Leon didn't know about, we had to hire armed security guards to be at our office at all times. This was an expensive investment we did not have the money for, not to mention the way it detracted from the positive and inspiring atmosphere we tried so hard to create at our office. We were all looking over our shoulders constantly in fear—as we arrived at and departed from the office, while driving home, and even in our homes. It was an awful feeling for me personally, but I also carried the weight of my staff, who were experiencing this as well. Another example in learning to let go. If we know we are doing all we possibly can to protect ourselves, we have to leave the rest in God's hands and choose to not let fear win.

Have you ever looked in the mirror and asked yourself, "Who is that person?" You barely recognize yourself because you're so depleted, and yet somehow, you ended up here. You've been trying to run a marathon at a sprinter's pace. You've become someone you never wanted to be.

I've had many of these moments during my time with The Giving Keys. Then something wonderful happens, and I'm inspired all over, and I get back up and try again.

Something wonderful, like our beloved Ramona. We hired her through one of our nonprofit partners, like Leon, as she was also transitioning out of homelessness. Ramona worked for us for three years. She was part of our family. Imagine a soft-spoken, sweet grandma who wears pearls and glasses, who cries every day at the drop of a hat because she's so touched by how grateful she is to have a job that's changing her life.

Then, out of nowhere, Ramona went missing. She and her best friend at work, Betty, took the same bus home every day. Betty said she'd parted from Ramona the night before the same way she normally does, and everything had seemed fine. Days went by wherein we didn't hear anything. We called the people she lived with, and they hadn't seen her in days, either. We were alarmed and confused. It didn't add up. We genuinely assumed she was dead. Our minds were spinning, and we began imagining all sorts of things that could have happened. Everyone in the office was devastated, crying and overwhelmed, wondering what had happened to her.

The week after she'd been missing a whole week, we brought in grief and trauma counselors for each of our employees to meet with, including me—even though I fully realized that this expense, on top of hired armed security guards, was not in the budget for our little giveback jewelry company. When you're the boss, you just do what you need to do.

Another week went by, and we never heard a word about Ramona. And then, on a Friday afternoon, she showed up at the office. We were shocked and asked where she'd been. Was she OK? What had happened? She said she was there to get her paycheck. She'd relapsed on her crack addiction and needed the money to pay back the drug dealer. Her elderly mother had kicked her out of her house, so she was back on Skid Row. (Skid Row is the place in downtown LA with thousands of tents sprawled on the streets, containing one of the largest populations of people experiencing homelessness in the United States, and has been known for its condensed homeless population with its long history of drugs and police raids since the 1930s.)

We couldn't believe what we were hearing. This wasn't the Ramona we knew.

Our director of impact called all the inpatient and outpatient rehab facilities in the surrounding area, but everything was maxed. Even if we had pushed, there was so much red tape to get through. No wonder so many people in the thick of their addictions can't find a way out. Even our team, including our highly educated director of impact with her master's degree and numerous LA nonprofit connections, couldn't figure out a way to get Ramona the help she so desperately needed. It's such a broken system. (Side note: I hope hearing this creates more grace and understanding, *and even passion, for the injustice of it—for the people who are essentially trapped on the streets.)*

Thankfully, after calling in favors, we finally got connected to the right person at the LA Mission, and they found a spot for Ramona! It was a year-long, live-in rehabilitation program. We told her we would hold her job for her *if* she completed the full year and graduated. Thank God, she agreed. She completed the year, graduated, and is back on our production team. She's assembling jewelry and stronger than ever. But let me tell you, this one experience really took it out of all of us. The whole team. Was the work we were doing—giving people a second chance, an opportunity to get their feet under them—wasted if someone relapsed? Thankfully, Ramona's story is one of healing and overcoming, but sadly, we have many other stories of beloved team members that don't end like Ramona's.

One Sunday morning, a few friends who went to Mosaic Church on Hollywood Boulevard (the same church where I'd met Colin) noticed a handsome young boy sleeping outside the church door. They'd started seeing him at services, and one day after church, they offered to take him to lunch. They came to learn his name— Cameron. They found out he was only nineteen years old and living on the streets. He told them he wanted to stay as close to the church as possible.

My friends immediately called me to ask if I could interview him for a job. We brought him in and fell in love with him right away. He had this beautiful, bright spirit about him, which I learned was a stark contrast to his heartbreaking story.

His birth mother was a drug addict (meth and crack, to be exact). She used while she was pregnant with Cameron, so he was born with the drugs in his system. He was born addicted. Because of this, Cameron's growing-up years were tough. He ended up in the foster care system and didn't have much stability in his life. When we met Cameron, his dream was to become a model. He started working at The Giving Keys and became part of our family, quite literally. We often invited him to lunch, my husband took him and some of the other guys on staff to a couple of Dodger games, and we always made a point to check in on him. We believe it's important to foster community with our staff, and our employees with especially traumatic backgrounds, like Cameron, craved—and deserved—the love and attention they'd been deprived of their whole lives.

One morning, I saw that Cameron had posted on Facebook that he was quitting his job at The Giving Keys. It was odd. The message didn't really make sense, so it was a red flag that maybe he'd relapsed and was high while writing it. Our team scrambled and tried to offer the best support we could. It was a roller-coaster ride trying to help him get sober. He was in multiple programs: Celebrate Recovery and Covenant House, among others. But he still decided to leave The Giving Keys. Of course, we were sad to lose one of our beloved staff members, but we were even more sad to see him relapse and struggle to find his way again.

Overall, here's what I've learned: you can't change people. You can be there for them. You can do research and provide options to support them, but they have to want it. Addiction is the individual's disease that no outside person can cure. Sobriety has to be personal. The individual has to be willing. He or she has to want to change.

It's not easy to spend your life wanting to help hurting people. You fall in love with them, and then you lose them. They come back—may even seem like they're back for good—and then you lose them again.

The last time I ever saw Cameron, I was eating at Marmalade Cafe at The Grove in Los Angeles. I looked up from my food to see the best sight I could imagine: he was working there as a server. We were both ecstatic to see each other. We hugged and gushed and took pictures together. I felt so proud and relieved to see him looking so put-together and responsible. I left filled with joy and gratitude, knowing The Giving Keys was able to be a starting point for Cameron, that it had been a launching pad for him. One of our goals is to be a "bridge employer"—a company that can bridge the gap between homelessness and helping our staff find careers they love.

We don't need to be the end game for our staff. We're thrilled to be a stepping stone. Seeing Cameron that day felt like *yes*, this is what it's all about.

But that day at Marmalade Cafe wasn't the end of the story. One night, a few months later, my heart broke. Really broke. I was lying in bed, casually scrolling through Facebook (as you do), and there it was: "R.I.P. Cameron." My heart dropped down to my stomach. I sat straight up in bed and started scouring Facebook, looking at mutual friends' pages, to see if it was really true. It was true. I started bawling hysterically. Like deep, guttural crying. How could this be? I had just seen him! He had seemed so alive. He had seemed so happy and healthy.

I later found out that he had relapsed and died a very gruesome death, alone. This is the hard stuff. This is the stuff I never knew I was signing up for. Sometimes, when we pray that prayer to feel what God might feel for people, heartbreak is part of the deal. Heartbreak is bound to happen when we let ourselves *really* love people.

I've learned that when you step out to do something important and impactful, everything that comes with it is that much harder. The high joys and gutting lows all come with the territory. And ultimately, it's a gift. What a gift to be a part of Cameron's life. What a gift to call him friend. What a gift to be a little part of his story and to make a positive impact in his life on this earth. I will never recover from losing him, but it was such a gift to know him.

His adopted mother reached out and asked to get his name engraved on some Giving Keys. They were passed out at his funeral. It was so surreal to see his name on the very product he helped to create—a symbol of so much hope and healing—now looking like a symbol of loss, grief, and sadness.

When something matters so deeply to you, you inevitably open yourself up to being hurt. When you love deeply, the losses cut just as deep. You can't save everyone. As much as you can love and care for someone, you can't rescue them from their own dark struggle. All you can do is show up, be there, and love them hard.

Living your purpose will always be a mix of hard knocks and rewarding wins. That's why extra grace and grit is always required. I saw this play out on our team and in our company in so many ways.

It's important to me that our employees have the best support and resources possible available to them. It's also critical that we hire well so people will like where they work, do good work, and enjoy working with one another. So it can be challenging when you find out someone on your team is not clicking.

Which brings me to Lana, queen bee of the office mean girls.

Word got to me that Lana, one of our product development employees, had a very vocal and toxic attitude. She was new to the fashion and social enterprise industries, and while she had lots of heart, her good intentions combined with her critical attitude made for a sour combo. Her negativity began affecting the morale of the team, and work relationships were becoming strained.

I learned Lana was gossiping about The Giving Keys leadership team—me included—to everyone in the company (and probably beyond). People were feeling like she was trying to turn them against us with her judgmental opinions. So naturally, I wanted to get to the bottom of this.

Finally, one day she explained in an email that she thought we (the leadership team) were focusing too much and caring about marketing and not enough on our production employees who are transitioning out of homelessness, among many other skewed views.

The nice way to say this: Lana's heart may have been in the right place, but unfortunately, she didn't know or see the whole picture. How I really felt: It was incredibly maddening to read her opinions, and by the end of it, my blood was boiling. How dare she accuse us of not caring enough?! She hadn't seen me bawling in my bed at night because I care TOO much.

Here's the thing. Lana was in product development, so she was in the meetings where we talked about jewelry, the metals, and the designs. She wasn't in any of the meetings, or on the hundreds of phone calls, or involved in the behind-the-scenes efforts where the leadership team and I were wracking our brains trying to do everything we possibly could to help our dozens of production associates, like Ramona and Cameron.

I felt like I had to defend myself. And I sure tried to. But then I realized this was just another instance where I needed to let go and detach. I can't control what Lana or anyone else thinks of me, so I shouldn't let her or anyone else's opinions sway me or influence my emotional balance or my view of myself. But it's often hard to do this.

After Lana expressed her concerns and I put effort into explaining the bigger picture to her, things seemed like they'd be better. But then we had another issue.

It was Lana's responsibility to manage the relationship with an outsourced jewelry designer we worked with named Shelley Gibbs, who now owns The Last Line, a fabulous luxury diamond jewelry company. We headed into the weekend knowing we had a meeting scheduled with Shelley on Monday morning at 11 a.m. But Shelley emailed both Lana and me on Saturday, asking if she could move our important meeting to 9 a.m. on Monday instead of 11 a.m. as originally planned. Not a big deal, but we obviously needed to connect that weekend to make sure the time change worked for everyone. Our office hours opened back up at 9 a.m. Monday morning across town so I knew Lana couldn't see the email in time unless I texted her.

Though it was Lana's responsibility to manage the relationship and meeting with Shelley, I had a feeling she might not see the email since it was Saturday morning (and of course, as the boss, I check my work inbox 24/7), so I sent her a quick text.

I asked if she could make the meeting time Shelley had requested. She didn't respond. So I texted her again on Sunday, saying, "Hey, just making sure you saw my text yesterday as Shelley has requested to move our meeting tomorrow morning earlier. I wanted to see if you can do that." She replied that it was unacceptable for me to contact her on the weekend, even though she was a salaried employee. She proceeded to say she'd had a wedding to attend that weekend and was spending time with her family.

Now, let me be extremely clear here. It's very important to me that our staff has a healthy work/life balance. There should be boundaries with work, and our people should turn off their phones and enjoy their weekends. It's important, and so often in our culture, the need for balance is disregarded or modeled poorly, so people don't actually feel they can take a break. So I make it a top priority to *not* contact employees after hours on weekdays and especially not on weekends. They should have a break from work, and they deserve it. I have always respected that and think it's not only important to uphold that value, but it's also vital that I set the example as the boss. I want my staff to feel they can actually enjoy their lives and recharge.

That said, there are exceptions that come up sometimes that are out of our control. I felt this particular situation was a reasonable exception, given the importance of this particular meeting and the timing of our partner's request. Not to mention, I was not asking Lana to do any work over the weekend. I simply needed her to respond with a "yes" or a "no" so I could write Shelley back and confirm, or organize another day for us to meet.

Little did I know the can of worms I opened up that weekend. Lana decided to take to Facebook and post her rant. Of course, she was Facebook friends with all of The Giving Keys employees, including me, but that didn't hold her back. She posted something to the effect of, "Isn't it frustrating when your employer doesn't let you have time off or vacation time, then disrespects your time off and just expects you to work around the clock?" To top it off, she then posted a link about a hugely successful, billion-dollar company that offers unusually generous time off, vacation time, and other perks.

Once again, Lana had me fuming with rage. She took a small situation, twisted it, then ranted publicly about her skewed perspective of what happened. I immediately wrote a scathing (but brilliant, if I do say so myself) public response to her Facebook post, but then our president urged me to delete it. I regained my composure and did so. The phrase "entitled millennial" may have been included in my frustrated rant to my husband afterward . . . Let's just say that relationship did not end well.

Another thing I've learned being the boss: You can't please everybody. It's literally impossible. And trust me, I've tried. Really hard.

We hired a girl who was one of the best administrative employees we'd ever had. She was in charge of our events. Meet Taylor, admin angel. She had the brightest personality, and I had total peace of mind knowing she was out in the field representing The Giving Keys.

But at some point, I started to sense that she was getting overwhelmed and flustered. I could tell she wasn't "all in" anymore. So I began to be extra attentive, affirming, and encouraging to her. After she had worked a long weekend of events for us, I bought her a gift certificate for a massage. A nice gesture, of course, but then I realized I was acting more like a wooing boyfriend than an employer.

Then, it dawned on me that I didn't just behave this way with Taylor. I was constantly trying to tap dance, to woo our employees by doing all the things a boyfriend would do—compliment them on how beautiful they were, compliment their outfits, constantly check up on them and ask how they're doing, buy them gifts, to keep them happy and keep them at The Giving Keys. It was exhausting. When Taylor finally ended up quitting, I remember feeling like she was legitimately breaking up with me. I'm not kidding. I saw her at the office the day after I'd heard the news via email. We looked at each other, and we both cried and hugged. She kept saying things like, "I love you, and I love The Giving Keys. There are just other things I want to explore in my life and career," which I knew was true. But after trying so hard to retain her, it still felt like a defeat. I know people have to move on to their next adventure and follow their career goals, but it still felt strangely like the "It's not you, it's me" breakup moment. It triggered feelings of rejection in me. Another reason why bosses need to get emotionally healthy—note to self.

Our entire production team loved, respected, and relied on Erin, our production manager. She was not only skilled at the technical side of her job, but she also did a beautiful job of working with, supporting, and championing our employees who were transitioning out of homelessness. It was like she was made for the job.

But Erin struggled to get along with some of the support staff, specifically the two people she had to work with the most. I tried to coach them through their conflicts. I even tried to take them to a girls' night out dinner together as an attempt to help them bond.

But these women kept coming to me, saying they were afraid of Erin because of the way she spoke and disrespected them. If you weren't on Erin's good side, they said, "You better watch out."

As much as we knew our production team loved Erin, we couldn't have bullying on the team, so we finally decided to let her go. We were honestly worried our production team, whom she managed and who loved her, might turn on us because of the decision. Erin was furious and refused to take responsibility for any of her actions. Later, after she'd left The Giving Keys, I found out she was pregnant, so I bought her baby girl a present. I was disappointed to learn she declined my gift, which I'd passed along via a mutual friend. I was shocked. Ouch. Olive branch swatted away. Once again, you can't please everyone. You have to just do your best with what you know and the full picture you see. Leading a company is no easy feat.

Then there was Darnell, "my favorite." Darnell was trying to transition out of homelessness, and I had a special connection with him from the start. When we hired him, he was incredibly confident and told us he'd be the best engraver we'd ever have.

And you know what? He was right. He really did have a special gift for his job. Whenever guests would come to the office, he would get an almost prophetic read on them. He'd always know the exact word to describe what they needed in their life at the time. I nicknamed him our "Wordsmith." People started coming to our office just to experience Darnell's gift. It was almost like people were coming to see a prophet, psychic, or tarot card reader. And when I say people started coming in, I mean all sorts of people. Big-time talent agents, housewives, celebrities. He always hit the nail right on the head (pun intended).

One time, a high-level producer came in but was pretty skeptical about Darnell's purported gift for wordsmithing. Darnell asked her a couple of questions and then engraved the word TAPESTRY for her. Initially, she looked a bit confused. Then he very confidently said, "You really hold it all together. You hold projects together. You hold people together. You hold yourself together. You hold it all together. Just like a tapestry. If it weren't for you, it would all fall apart." She literally started crying and said, "Wow, yes, you're 100 percent right on. Thank you from the bottom of my heart."

Darnell was a special soul, and he obviously held a special place on our team, but it wasn't all sunshine and roses. He was talented at his craft, but he struggled with mental health, being a team player, and being managed. His behavioral issues put a constant strain on the team, and his managers repeatedly wanted to fire him because of problems that continued to happen. I always defended him and had extra grace for him because I knew how much he had gone through and overcome.

Darnell watched his own father blow his brains out when he was only nine years old. So of course he had severe trauma, and of course he was going to have issues we should try and navigate through. Also, because he was still experiencing homelessness, of course he was going to have an impossible time getting hired anywhere else. So of course I was going to keep giving him chances to stay at The Giving Keys. If not here, where else would he go?

I fought for Darnell over and over again. It got to the point where our main production manager quit because he felt like I was choosing Darnell over him. He felt I was undermining him as Darnell's manager. That was a tough day. I understood how hard it was for him to manage Darnell, but I could always understand Darnell's point of view, too. I wanted to give him 77 chances forever because I deeply believe in second chances. It's a huge principle at The Giving Keys.

Every time I was faced with having to make the final decision about Darnell's employment, I would think of this parable in the Gospel of Luke. Jesus is talking to the disciples and says, "Suppose one of you has 100 sheep and loses one of them. Won't he leave the

99 in the open country? Won't he go and look for the one lost sheep until he finds it?" Darnell was always the one to me. And for better or worse, I would sacrifice it all for the one.

I even met with an investor who believed in The Giving Keys potential, and wanted to "blow us up" with all his money and ideas, but he said I would have to let go of caring so much about each "individual" like Darnell, and focus on the big picture if I really wanted to scale the company. I could never bring myself to be that "ambitious."

For his birthday one year, all Darnell wanted to do was show our director of impact, Bentley; our president, Brit; and I all the different dumpsters he used to sleep next to. I drove us all around Los Angeles, and he would say, "Turn right, turn left, go down this alley, see that dumpster right there? In that gate, yeah, I would always sleep right in between that dumpster and fence because it was safe. OK, turn right, turn left here, see that back alley in that door? That gate lifted up so I could sleep safely in that outside hallway." We were so taken aback, overwhelmed by the reality of where he came from and how far he had come from those days on the streets—and honored, too, that he wanted to share this significant piece of his life with us on his birthday.

When I had my first child, Brave, Darnell was the only person on our entire staff who got Brave a present. I tell this not to make everyone else from The Giving Keys who might be reading this feel bad, but to showcase Darnell's heart. He went to a nice jeweler downtown and had "Brave" professionally engraved on a real gold ID bracelet. It was so thoughtful and meant the world to me.

Drugs were not Darnell's kryptonite or downfall. It was drinking. After his fiancée broke up with him, he was deeply lonely. He admitted to me that on weekends, he drank too much and got into trouble. He got into fights and sometimes showed up to work with a bloodied face, black eye, and split lip. His phone was stolen over and over again when he was out drinking. He always had a different story to explain why. I had his name saved in my phone eight different times because of how many times he changed his number.

I wondered about Darnell's mental health sometimes, because on multiple occasions I received paranoid texts from him in the middle of the night—texts saying that people were outside his house, trying to kill him. It was always a challenge for me to know what to do and what to believe.

I even got my family involved. My husband, my dad, and I took him to lunch multiple times to try to coach him on how to respect his managers and fellow team members, as we continued to get complaints about him. I even brought my half-brother from Austin, Texas, to our office to share his sobriety story, hoping to inspire Darnell (and others). My brother was an addict for years, then became a drug counselor. They exchanged numbers and stayed in touch. Still, Darnell's struggles persisted.

I finally had to draw the line. I had repeatedly begged him to be respectful and given him multiple ultimatums. But one day, when he was getting some feedback from a supervisor on how he could perform better, he said " F%$#@ y'all," flipped off the team, and walked out. This, combined with learning that our new production manager was going to quit because of Darnell *and* our other production employees didn't feel safe around him finally tipped the scales. The team expressed that they felt we weren't being fair because they abided by our expectations, but Darnell didn't have to follow the rules because he was *my* "favorite." I knew what I had to do. It was time to let Darnell go.

Letting someone go is never easy, but that was a particularly hard day. I took Darnell to coffee with our president and HR lead and watched him sign his final paperwork. We stayed in touch for a while, but I'm sad to say he must've changed his phone number again. I've been unable to get ahold of him lately. I felt like Darnell was a family member, so it breaks my heart that he's not in my life anymore. Now I just pray that he gets the help he needs and that he'll be OK. I'm even tearing up writing this. As much as I can keep reiterating "detach with love," as I learned in my Al-Anon group, and it sounds good in principle, it can be excruciating to let go of someone you care about.

Live long enough, and sooner or later, you will love someone deeply and get hurt by them. But it's like they say—would you rather have never loved at all? I say no. Whether you're looking around and seeing all the brokenness in this world, trying to figure out how to be part of a solution, watching a friend or family member struggle with addiction, or you've been in a relationship that broke your heart, the deep love is real and the deep pain is just as real.

It turned out I had a lot more to learn about love, because as invested as I was in loving others, I didn't realize I was neglecting self-love. I was so busy taking care of people, I had given up on taking care of myself.

As my health deteriorated from the demands and stress, I mostly ignored it, thinking I had to keep my focus on the mission that mattered. But if you don't fill your own tank, you can't get very far, no matter how noble your aims are.

Unfortunately, since starting The Giving Keys, I've had to go to the ER on multiple occasions because of heart pain. I found out I have a rare heart condition called mitral valve prolapse, which causes heart murmurs. When my stress level gets too high, I feel pain in my heart. Before I knew about my condition, every time I experienced this pain, I thought I was having a heart attack.

Another part of owning a company and being a boss is outsourcing support and relying on consultants to help make big business decisions. When someone on your internal team, someone you're supposed to trust, disagrees with the outside advisors, it's extremely confusing and difficult to navigate. I've felt pulled in opposite directions and unsure who to trust on multiple occasions. For example, we experienced an ongoing conflict between one of our consultants and a vital person on my team about our taxes—how to file them, how much it would cost us, and so on. I was torn. I'd hired *both* parties to help me make wise decisions, and when they didn't see eye-to-eye, I was confused and felt caught in the middle. In this particular situation—and it's like a punch in the gut to tell you this—the conflict led to a mistake that ultimately cost us six figures. We're still trying to recover from it today. This threw me into a full panic attack, which landed me in the ER again.

I was on multiple calls one day, trying to ease the tension between these two parties who disagreed about the taxes. I was trying to get us all on the same page, and I knew they were both frustrated with me for not trusting them. That's when the heart pains started to get really bad.

I didn't want to go back to the ER again, much less spend over $1,000 there, so I told my husband I needed him to take me to the beach. I thought maybe watching the waves would calm me down. We went to one of my favorite restaurants, Moonshadows, which is right on the water. Surely seeing and hearing the waves crash and catching the sunset would reduce my stress and heart pain. Why not a shot of tequila, too? I figured it wouldn't hurt.

But the panic and pain did not subside, so I ended up in urgent care. The doctor there explained the side effects of my condition. He told me I needed to get a better hold on the stress in my life, otherwise, as I get older, it *will* turn into a heart attack.

I sat in that urgent care and thought to myself, *How? There's no way to reduce the stress I carry with owning and running The Giving Keys. It's too big and complex.* I genuinely didn't think I could ever figure out a way to *not* be so stressed. It just seemed like par for the course. This is what happens when you run a business. You're overwhelmed and constantly going. People always need you. You're never "off," always "on."

In the opening chapters, I talked about how important it is to keep your eyes open for opportunities to give. And it may sound like I'm taking all of that back in sharing about the hardship that can come along with that. I found a quote from the Talmud that I feel represents a nice balance of both sides:

> Do not be daunted by the enormity of the world's grief. Do justly now, love mercy now, walk humbly now. You are not obligated to complete the work, but neither are you free to abandon it.

I realized the only way to survive and thrive in leadership is by shifting to a service mentality. My pastor, Joseph Barkley, said this in one of his sermons: "Don't serve at the rate of return. Serve at the level of love. We don't serve or lead with excellence because we get a reward. We serve because people are worth it."

I still had lessons to learn on the way to a level of service leadership that is sustainable, one that wouldn't land me in the ER or come at great personal expense. But I was starting to see that my first order of business was to get my priorities straight. If I truly wanted to serve others, I had to start by taking care of myself so that I was serving from a healthy place.

The Scriptures teach us to love our neighbors as ourselves. But how can we love others well if we skip the first step of loving and caring for ourselves?

chapter eight

SAVE YOUR SAVIOR COMPLEX

The wound is the place where
the light enters you.

—Rumi

As I've told you, I grew up praying for my future husband. I dreamed of the perfect man for me. He'd be my person to laugh with, cry with, build a family and enjoy life together with. I'll admit, it actually felt like that in the beginning of my relationship with Colin.

But anyone who's been in a relationship past the honeymoon phase knows it's bound to change over time. Life gets real, and early in my first pregnancy, Colin and I hit a low-low moment.

I have to preface this story by saying that I was extremely pregnant and extremely hormonal. This isn't an excuse for the behavior I'm about to describe to you, but I hope it gives you a fuller picture (and maybe incites you to extend me a little bit of extra grace).

One day, Colin and I got in a pretty heated argument. To this day, I don't remember what we fought about, which tells you how important it was, but at the time it felt like the ultimate thing to be fighting about. Like a hill you'd die on if you had to—because hormones.

Anyway, while I was putting all my energy and attention into this fight I was having with Colin, I wasn't paying attention to the fact that I was holding my phone. In fact, what was *open* on my phone was a text thread with my entire Giving Keys leadership staff—the president, COO, director of marketing, director of product development, and director of HR. I'd been sending updates to the group regarding progress on a project. This, I'm sorry to say, was a pretty accurate picture of how I was living my life at that point: only half-present with what was happening in front of me, and half-present with the work I felt obligated to attend to.

So I was holding my phone, not paying attention, and the fight was getting more and more heated. It was one of those ugly fights where your emotions get the best of you and you say things you regret. Well, somehow, I unknowingly pressed the voice memo button on the text thread, which recorded the climax of our fight.

It wasn't until the fight was over and I was outside that I heard it—that familiar "whoop" sound your phone makes when it sends a message. My heart dropped. I looked down at my phone, and to my great horror, I saw that a *minute-long* voice memo of my fight with Colin had just been sent to my entire leadership team. You can't make this stuff up.

I frantically hoped that it was just a minute of silence recorded as I walked to the car. But then I pressed play and heard our voices as clear as day. Colin yelled, "Caitlin, you're acting crazy!" I screamed back at the top of my lungs, "Oh, that's *great* that you're calling your pregnant wife crazy!" The recording ended with me yelling some choice words I hope my children never hear me repeat (God help me). Then—because life is hilarious and cruel—you could hear the resolute, unapologetic slamming of the front door.

I could not believe it. My heart was pounding. My face was red, even though no one was there to see. I was completely mortified. I had worked *so* hard to be a leader, to live by example, and to keep up the appearance that I knew what I was doing—to be a shiny CEO. The truth is, I was trying to be the "savior" both at work and at home. And now none of it mattered. I would be known for who I was behind closed doors.

I immediately deleted the voice memo even though, deep down, I knew it wouldn't help matters since it had already been delivered. My whole body shook in a panic, as I wrote the fastest text I'd ever written: "Please, I'm begging you, do *not* listen to that voice memo! I accidentally sent it, and it's of me and my husband fighting. Please. I'm begging you with everything in me to *not* press play and immediately delete it!" I can only imagine what everyone was thinking (and of course, looking back, I think, *What is the first thing you want to do when someone tells you "don't listen to that"? You want to listen to it, of course!*)

No one responded.

Cringe.

Hearing nothing back made my head spin with anxiety about what everyone was thinking. They were probably so uncomfortable.

When it came to being a boss, I tried with everything in me to be an honorable, caring leader. Someone people would want to work for. I tried to keep it all together and be strong for them. Even when everything in me was about to explode, I tried to be helpful and bring solutions, not problems, to work. But the voice memo was just one example that showed me—and my staff—my weakness, my flaws, with no filter. It was a hard pill to swallow.

Every time I tried to lead the way I *thought* a leader would lead, and do it perfectly, I fell on my face. Yet I found that when I gave myself permission to lead imperfectly, to let my vulnerability and flaws show, I actually started believing I was up for the job.

When that voice memo went out to my leadership team, I had no choice but to own it and surrender to how raw it was. Surrender to being imperfect. That I struggle with demons just like everyone else. It's not always easy to admit something like that, and I didn't have the guts to even mention it again until months later (I think shame has a way of creeping in, lingering, and growing unless it's outed), but I've learned it's where freedom lies—in admitting our humanity to one another.

There's a common complex, especially among people who are a mixture of compassionate, resourceful, driven, and have a natural empathy for those who are less fortunate. It's called the savior complex. It's a posture wherein someone is trying to be the hero, the savior. It often creeps in where someone has a genuine desire to do good in the world. The trouble comes when we forget that we are flawed and in need of help or improvement/growth in some way. Sure, we can help people; that's not bad per se. But we need to remember that we are all broken in different ways. Perhaps, when you think you're helping others, they might be the ones helping you. I'm becoming more convinced of this over time.

My inspiring friend, Mike Foster, eloquently said, "We are always both the patient and the physician in our work. However, many leaders don't acknowledge how they are the patient too. Our work helps in our own healing." Mike is a social entrepreneur who leads People of the Second Chance, helping individuals turn their setbacks into superpowers.

One of my best friends, Kim Biddle, who founded the nonprofit Saving Innocence to help end child sex trafficking, once told me, "One of the most vulnerable expressions of philanthropy is when we turn our own pain and suffering into something beautiful to help and empower others. I may never see justice brought against the men who sexually abused me as a child, or for the human beings who were purchased for sexual acts, but I could take my broken heart and try to create a world that is safer for us all to live in."

She warned me, however. "This road of redemption is sneaky," she said. "It reveals in you new layers of healing that must take place in order for mercy to coexist with the fight for justice. There is a temptation to neglect my own heart and healing for the sake of running after the world's healing, as if the world was more my responsibility than my own well-being. But without the internal healing and transformation, true justice and freedom is never fully attained. Love and compassion are as important to learn for ourselves as they are for our neighbor. These must coexist if the world is going to be restored to its fullest version."

It's a beautiful, meant-to-be manifestation when we are given the opportunity to go through a painful journey; gather real, deep, empathetic wisdom; develop a bleeding heart about the issue; then take all of that and let it overflow onto others who are going through something similar. I think that the attachment of our own pain to the cause we are fighting for is crucial in order to prevent pride from creeping in. Because we know we've been there, too.

For instance, in starting Love Your Flawz, I was naturally passionate about encouraging others to love their own flaws because I desperately needed to love mine. And seeing other people learn to love their flaws helped me learn to love mine.

I needed (and still need) all the words on The Giving Keys. In hindsight, I think I subconsciously needed a deeper, more tangible way to practice loving my flaws in my daily life. Wearing all the different scarred-up rusty, broken, imperfect shapes and sizes was a daily reminder. Keys are the symbols of opening and closing. A key can represent freedom, or it can represent incarceration. Keys give us security, which I also desperately needed. All the words I needed on these keys became a recipe for healing, both for me and for the million-plus people who have been given keys around the world.

When I sent that voice memo to my leadership team, it was my face-to-the-pavement moment to evaluate and decide on the kind of leader I wanted to be and the kind of company I wanted to build. I had to remember that The Giving Keys isn't about *us* helping *them*. It's about all of us helping each other. Shining lights on each other. Healing each other.

We've done some work with Homeboy Industries (which employs ex-gang members) founding director Father Gregory Boyl. I think he explains this beautifully:

> I thought I could "save" gang members. I was wrong. We cannot turn the light switch on for anyone. But we all own flashlights. With any luck, on any given day, we know where to aim them for each other. We do not rescue anyone at the margins. But go figure, if we stand at the margins, we are all rescued.

Even before the voice memo occurrence, the entire Giving Keys team had already been pretty awe-inspiring at supporting and being real with each other. Nikki and Kelly, two production employees at The Giving Keys, were models of this from the beginning. They had a gift for knowing when I was having a rough day. If I strolled into work with a plastered-on smile, they could sense I was going through something behind closed doors, and one of them always walked over to me and gave me the biggest hug.

The redemptive, beautiful thing about it was that these women had been to hell and back. They'd experienced so much darkness, yet there they saw me, the person behind their employer and boss. They were a source of comfort, perspective, and healing. No words were needed. The hug always said it all. These are the things money can't buy. And with it, they were helping me more than I was helping them. From Skid Row to 9021(1), we all need each other.

Then there's Robert, who is in his fifties and was incarcerated for most of his life. He's one of the most incredible and wise people I've ever met.

One Monday I asked him, "How was your weekend?"

He said, "Oh, it was good. I went to Disneyland this weekend."

"Oh nice!" I said. " What was your favorite ride?"

"Oh no," he explained. "I didn't go in. I just took the bus there and looked at it from outside, and it was incredible. And then I took the bus back home. It was a great weekend."

This kind of stuff is medicine for my soul. I needed to hear that! I needed to be reminded of how simple it can be to be happy. There are so many things I take for granted—that we *all* take for granted.

Another day, I asked Robert, "How was your day?"

"It was great," he said. "I went to the DMV."

I giggled a little bit to myself, because whoever says the words "great" and "DMV" in the same sentence? Especially in LA, where you can spend over half a day just waiting in line. Everybody usually declares with dread "Ahh, I have to go to the DMV today." It's *the thing* to complain about.

But Robert went on.

"You know what? I went to the DMV and waited in line for my

ID, and I looked around and thought to myself, 'Wow, this place is amazing.'"

Again, medicine for my soul.

I asked him what was so amazing about the DMV, and he said waiting in line that day taught him about the virtue of patience. He realized life is a lot like the DMV—it's not the line that matters but how you wait that makes the difference.

Robert, you're an angel genius. Be still my heart.

Kelly, Nikki, and Robert have all been through unspeakable things. And more often than not, they're the ones who are teaching me, inspiring me, encouraging me, making the job I do worth doing every day.

So go ahead and save your savior complex. No one's asking for it, anyway.

We can't do any of this alone, I'm learning. We need each other. I love this Scripture from 1 Corinthians 12:19–26 that perfectly describes how we're all unique and why we need one another:

> If all the parts were the same, how could there be a body? As it is, there are many parts. But there is only one body.
>
> The eye can't say to the hand, "I don't need you!" The head can't say to the feet, "I don't need you!" In fact, it is just the opposite. The parts of the body that seem to be weaker are the ones we can't do without. The parts that we think are less important we treat with special honor. The private parts aren't shown. But they are treated with special care. The parts that can be shown don't need special care. But God has put together all the parts of the body. And he has given more honor to the parts that didn't have any. In that way, the parts of the body will not take sides. All of them will take care of one another. If one part suffers,

every part suffers with it. If one part is honored, every part shares in its joy.

The savior complex doesn't work at the office or at home. It doesn't work successfully anywhere, really, because we relate the most when we're able to acknowledge the fullness of our existence—faults and all.

I was on a flight from LA to DC to go to the highly powerful and prestigious United States Institute Of Peace, to give a speech right after US presidential candidate Cory Booker. I was feeling overwhelmed. Mid-flight, I texted Colin and told him what was on my mind—that I felt pressure to be inspiring to all these people. It was weighing on me, and I was feeling ill-equipped, like I didn't have much left to give. He texted me back and simply said, "We don't need more heroes. We need more humans."

In that instant, it was like the pressure lifted. I didn't need to be the hero. The Giving Keys didn't need to be the hero. Our employees didn't need to be heroes. The people I was about to speak to didn't need to be heroes. We all just need to be human—to be real, honest, and authentic with one another—as we walk through this unpredictable experience called life. It's hard enough to be human, let alone try to carry the weight of being a hero for everyone.

What would our world look like if we focused on loving people well rather than swooping in with our red capes? What would our marriages and families look like? What would our places of work look like?

You are qualified because you are human. That's more than enough.

Shortly after that tragic voice memo to my leadership team—I found out that Oprah had chosen me for her SuperSoul 100 list. Oprah's SuperSoul 100 list is, according to her website, "A collection of 100 awakened leaders who are using their voices and talent to elevate humanity." I was, of course, taken aback and honored to be selected.

And that's when I witnessed firsthand just how much *more* is possible when you are willing to lead as a human and not as a superhero.

One of the first events we were invited to participate in was the chance to meet Oprah and the other 99 people on the list. I don't think I have to explain to you how excited I was to meet the one and only Oprah, the queen herself. She had pristine hair and makeup and was wearing a bright, colorful, flowy dress to match her bright, colorful essence. I was both ecstatic and nervous as I walked into the lobby of her office, which was filled with the most inspirational people in the world.

Oprah had a full brunch buffet set up in the lobby (did I mention I was pregnant at the time?), so basically, I died and went to heaven. I mean, come on, being in Oprah's presence *and* an all-you-can-eat buffet?! Thank you, Lord.

I remember coming back to my seat next to Yael Cohen—she started F&$! Cancer and is married to Scooter Braun, who manages Justin Bieber and Ariana Grande. I had filled my plate with a loaded bagel. One side of the bagel was weighed down with cream cheese and strawberry jam, and the other side of the bagel had a ton of cream cheese and a gallon of onions. Because strawberries and onions make a great combination, right?

Yael looked at my plate and said, "Wow, you really are pregnant."

Probably one of my favorite things about the day was seeing how normal Oprah is. It may sound strange, but it was refreshing to see her eat food; interact with her partner, Stedman Graham; and mingle around the room like the rest of us. It occurred to me as I watched Oprah that day that *Oprah* is a human, too. It was a reminder that, no matter what kind of work you do or your status in the world, everybody goes home at the end of the day and is left alone with their humanity—the fame, frills, and makeup removed.

While everyone else was dressed up, Stedman was in a casual tracksuit. This did not seem to faze either of them at all. In fact, I remember thinking, *While we're here fawning over the legend who has invited us to her office, from his point of view, this is probably just another event he's supposed to attend to support her.* It made me think of Colin's point of view when it comes to The Giving Keys and all of the events that includes. I knew he must feel like that a lot of the time. Watching how they interacted was another reminder to me that even *Oprah* is human.

And if Oprah is human, *everyone* is human!

As we ate and chatted with our fellow SuperSoul 100s, one of Oprah's producers told her it was time to share a little bit with us. She stood up with her mouth full and said, "Wait, but I just started eating this deviled egg!" I don't know what I expected her to do, but I was surprised by how relatable she was. She was just a normal person trying to eat her deviled egg, gosh dangit.

She then told us she wanted to support us and our endeavors. She said she thought of us as the people who were pushing light forth into the world. She said we were all there because we're doing things she is passionate about and wants to get behind. From her wildly famous talk shows, to her own magazine, to her own network, to her philanthropy, to her $6 billion net worth, to half the country wanting her to be president, I was in awe.

There were several group photos, and then we each got an opportunity to take individual photos with Oprah. I awkwardly waited and watched while everyone took turns having their photo taken. Life coach Mastin Kipp and I traded cell phones and pictures of us getting our picture taken with Oprah, so we didn't have to wait to get the pics back from the professional photographer. We needed instant gratification, people. And yes, we both took about a hundred pics of the same pose and looked at them all a hundred times.

When it was finally my turn, I walked up to her and stuck out my hand, with a huge grin across my face.

"Hi, I'm Caitlin," I said. "I do The Giving Keys."

"I know who you are!" Oprah declared as she went in for a hug. Her hug felt like butter. Or warm, fresh, soft chocolate chip cookies. And milk. And glitter.

We then posed for a photo together, and I don't think I've ever smiled bigger. She placed her hand on my pregnant belly, and I think Brave received the ultimate forever blessing, basically just as if the pope had blessed him. (No disrespect to the pope, as he's THE MAN and I 100 percent want him to bless my babies too, pretty please.)

Leaving the event that day, I was on a high. The opportunities seemed endless, and I felt ready to conquer the world. I Ubered home with the biggest smile on my face.

Then it was back to real life.

I walked into my dimly lit house. Colin was lying on the couch, watching golf. Things were still tense between us. We said hi, but I could tell we weren't really connected. I dropped my purse and sat down on the other side of the couch. I looked down at my phone, where I could see that my inbox was piling up with work emails as usual. My high began fading fast. I slumped down into the cushions and thought, *This is my actual life*. It doesn't matter how many incredible mountain-top experiences you have, how many once-in-a-lifetime events you're invited to, how many incredible world-changing things you do. At the end of the day, you go home to the people you love and that is your real life. That is the real you. What is most important and valuable to you? What are your priorities?

What are you going to do about it?

I was about to find out.

During one of the dark periods in my marriage, I left to go on an elite, by-invitation-only Summit Series cruise. There was a whole host of inspiring speakers there to teach and equip us, including the relationship guru, Esther Perel. One thing I found ironic was that, despite the fact that this trip was *filled* with top entrepreneurs and CEOs—speakers like Jeff Bezos, Amazon's founder and CEO; Jessica Alba, actress and founder of The Honest Company; and Martha Stewart—and there were plenty of lectures to choose from, the most packed sessions were always Esther's, the ones about relationships. The conference even had to add an extra session to the schedule because people were literally falling over each other to get in. I guess I wasn't the only business leader struggling with my romantic relationship.

Leading a business takes a toll on your relationships, and I took encouragement from the fact that I wasn't alone. I could still work to improve this part of my life.

One of the things Esther shared with us was that, if business owners treated their *romantic* partners like they treated business partners or employees, they would have much better relationships at home. She said that many of us business leaders give our all to our employees, then we come home, and our significant others get our leftovers.

As soon as I heard that, my heart sank. I knew it was true of my relationship with Colin. How must it feel to be Colin and be getting my leftovers? And by leftovers, I mean it was mostly that I was so exhausted and drained from work, I didn't have much to give by the time I got home.

There was no Wi-Fi on the boat, so if we wanted to check email, we had to wait in a long line to access the few computers they'd set up for attendees. Still, after Esther's session, I felt compelled to reach out to Colin. I wanted to tell him what I'd just heard and apologize to him for giving him my leftovers. I wanted to tell him I was ready to make it right. So I waited in that long line and wrote Colin a very short but heartfelt email. It simply said, "I really want to make this work. I love you, and I miss you. I'm sorry for all the things I have done to hurt you. I am in this for the long haul."

Of course, after that I was *dying* to see if Colin would write me back. We were supposed to be unplugging and taking time away from the internet, but every couple of hours, I would wait in the long line again to check my email for a message back from him. Finally, after my third or fourth trip through the line, I found the message I'd been waiting for. He told me he felt the same way and was sorry and wanted to make it work. It was so simple to apologize and commit to the effort. That's what we needed in order to start getting our feet back under us.

I smiled. We were going to make it. One day at a time.

Colin doesn't need me to save him, and I don't need him to save me. He doesn't need me to be a hero for him, but he *does* need me to be a human, real and vulnerable. Your friends and family need that from you, too. The world needs more of that from all of us. If we can give it, I believe the world will begin to transform into a safer, more beautiful place.

As Henri Nouwen writes, "Compassion means full immersion in the condition of being human."[*]

But there's more. It's not just about letting *ourselves* be human, but also about letting *other people* be human. We can only have compassion for others as much as we are able to practice compassion toward ourselves. So let's put down our critical magnifying glasses and judgment gavels, and let's all agree to be human together. Yes, of course, there comes a time when we need to rise up and challenge each other to be better and to do better, and to walk in our strength or "higher self," as some like to say. There is also a time to give people a break if they just don't have it in them right this minute. We can't control them, we can't manage them, and we can't save them. Anyway, maybe people don't want to be saved.

Ultimately, we can't help anyone if we are letting our self-care and self-compassion fall to the wayside.

There's a time to fight hard, to keep your passion to help alive, and there's also a time to let go. Your value does not come from how many people you help or how many you save. Your job description was never to be anyone's savior. Your only job description is to love with a love that surrenders any and all outcomes. You can't control those, but you can control how you engage and how you treat those around you.

Ready for the good news and the bad news?

Bad news first. Guess what? You're human. You will always be flawed. You will never entirely figure out this whole life business. You will fail, you will fall short, and you will make some splattered, colorful messes.

But here's the good news. You are HUMAN, which is another way of saying you are exactly what you were created to be. You are

---

[*] Henri Nouwen, *You Are the Beloved: Daily Meditations for Spiritual Living* (New York: Convergent, 2017), 244.

wonderfully and uniquely made. Your colorful messes are beautiful, because they're the colors of you. A work of art. A masterpiece. You were loved by God before you ever did anything impressive.

You are the one and only *you* this world has. You have a one-and-only soul. This is true for you and me as much as it's true for Oprah. Now *that's* some good news for all of us.

chapter nine

SCARRED & HARD

Never demean your scars, the fools will
laugh seeing them, only the wise will
know the reason behind them.

—Rumi

Just when The Giving Keys was really gathering steam, I got
a call from the White House. THE WHITE HOUSE, naturally.
It was an opportunity to speak at the Nexus Summit on the topic
of giving back, starting The Giving Keys, and social enterprise
and social impact. At first, I was over the moon, if a little anxious.
I hired a speaking coach to come work with me for a full day in
LA, convinced I was going to be more prepared for this speaking
engagement than I had ever been for any event in my life.

In an effort to make our tight timeline work, my coach took
a red-eye from Texas to LA and landed at 9 a.m., ready to spend
the entire day working with me until the speech was perfect. The
plan was for him to drive straight to my house from LAX for a full
day of coaching until he flew right back home that night. The only

problem was, when Sunday morning rolled around, I woke up feeling . . . well, not exactly like my best self.

At first I thought I could pull it together. I figured I must have eaten some bad sushi or something. But by the time his flight was on the ground, I was running to the bathroom every couple of minutes to throw up. I couldn't leave my house. I could barely make it off the bathroom floor.

Panicking a little, I texted this stranger speaking coach and asked if he could stall for an hour. I figured that would give me enough time to get my act together. And I kept thinking that if I could get some food in my stomach, I'd feel better. But everything I thought would make it better made it worse.

Suddenly it dawned on me. I should take a pregnancy test.

Because of all my health complications growing up, doctors always told me it would be difficult to have children. I always knew I wanted to have kids, but thanks to the messages I'd been fed over the years, I feared I would struggle to get pregnant or not be able to have kids at all.

Colin and I had worked our way into a good place, and a few months prior, I'd gone off my birth control pills to give my body a break and a chance to regulate itself.

But surely it wasn't possible to be pregnant this soon, after just three months of semi-trying?

Based on what the doctors had told me my whole life, I'd assumed it would take months, maybe even years, to get pregnant, if I got pregnant at all. I was relying on hope and prayer that a baby would come eventually. I really did believe it would be an "eventual" kind of thing.

As it turned out, it was an immediate kind of thing. Colin ran to the store to pick up tests for me, and as we watched the pink plus sign appear, we burst into tears with sheer excitement. It's one of my most treasured memories.

Meanwhile, as Colin and I were having our moment, my speaking coach was stalling at a Starbucks near my house, unsure what the heck was going on. I quickly regrouped, gave him a call, and told him the news. Yes, this stranger found out before our family and friends. I asked him to stall a little longer so we could FaceTime our families. He graciously understood, and finally came over about three hours after we had originally planned. Life does not always go the way you expect.

When he got there, I was still sick, so every few minutes I excused myself to run to the bathroom. I turned on our TV extra loud while I was gone so he couldn't hear me puking. I spent most of the day huddling under a blanket and don't remember much of anything about the entire session. I could not concentrate for the life of me.

But at this point—partly because I felt so miserable, and partly because I was so happy I was actually having a baby—an interesting thing started to happen. My priorities began to shift. My pattern started to shift. What had once seemed so important suddenly didn't seem important at all. Nothing in my speech seemed to matter anymore. God bless that coach of mine for his red-eye flight and efforts to coach me on such a wild day. Needless to say, that day came and went, and I didn't make any progress preparing for my speech at the White House.

Even though the session was a bomb, I still had a bit of time to prepare before the big presentation day. Then, things took another unexpected turn.

I went in for the standard prenatal tests but got word I was having a few pregnancy complications. My blood tests flagged some concerns and showed I needed to start medication to help avoid a miscarriage. I informed the doctor that I was booked to fly to Washington DC the following week to speak at the White House and wondered if that was still OK. She told me that while travel would normally be safe in the first trimester, because of my blood test results, the travel could possibly increase the chance of a miscarriage. It was OK to go but ultimately up to me.

"Wow, so it's just up to me?" I said, staring at her wide-eyed.

"Welcome to being a mother," she said.

Pregnancy comes with lots of firsts. Some of them you expect, but there were also plenty of "personal revelation firsts" that I didn't expect. I didn't expect to be so shocked by how hard I had pushed myself in the past—an approach I couldn't wisely continue to take now that I was growing a human life inside me. I didn't expect to say no to things that would have been such obvious yeses in the past. I *did* expect my body to change, but I didn't expect my heart and mind to change as much as it did.

I decided to cancel my speech at the White House. When it came down to it, the opportunity was not worth the slight risk. In this sense, growing new life inside me made my decision unbelievably easy. It was the first time I'd chosen my body, myself, my family over a groundbreaking career opportunity. And while there was definitely a part of me that felt sad to miss it, the greater feeling I had was *relief.* It was a gentle letting go of the way things used to be.

Though I felt relief because I wasn't as prepared as I had wanted to be for the speech, there was also the relief of saying no to something for the sake of my health and my baby's health. It was a big step for me to let go and realize I physically *can't* do everything. My body has limitations, and I have to honor those limitations. What a life-altering shift.

I was processing the deep realization that if I was going to be a mother, my patterns of work and pushing my body were going to have to change. In the past, I had worked extremely long hours in order to not only get the job done, but to try and spread our message and mission all over the world. I'm passionate about the work I do, so it never seemed like a stretch for me to work around the clock. Once I was pregnant, though, I quickly realized living this way wasn't going to work anymore.

As women, I think we have this tendency to feel like we can do everything. Or *should* do everything. Like we ought to be Wonder Woman and never have to draw boundaries or say no or take care of ourselves—that would be selfish or weak. But nothing could be further from the truth. Nothing could be more like the nurturing, strong, caring heart of a woman than to say "no" in order to protect her body, her baby, herself. And when I say "baby," I do not only mean a human baby which may or may not be growing inside you. I mean anything in your sphere that is depending on you for life. What are you nurturing?

You do not have to "push through." You do not have to keep hustling and grinding. There will always be pressure, and we can get ourselves into a mind-set where we really believe we don't have options. It's just *forward*, no matter the cost. Our bodies, our partners, our friends, our families, all suffer from this approach. God knows it's taken me a long time to have that first taste of, "It's OK to say no." It's OK to let things go.

When I look back on the first half of my journey with my breast issues (yes, there's more that will make your jaw drop) and everything that came along with it—learning to be a woman, paralyzing insecurity, worrying over if and who I would marry, wondering if I would ever become a mother—one constant theme was crippling fear. I know my fears came from valid causes, but I also know I let them have way too much power in my life. When you're trapped inside your fears, they are all-encompassing and appear to be never-ending. Even when one fear is overcome, we move on to the next one. Why do we do this?

There are probably a variety of reasons we become trapped in fear, especially fear related to things like femininity, motherhood, and marriage: survival mechanisms, pressure to live up to societal norms, learned behaviors and mind-sets, a mother's biological instinct to protect her child. A certain amount of fear is normal as it's a primitive human emotion. It alerts us to the presence of danger, and it was critical in keeping our ancestors alive. But it's important to not let fear rule our lives.

I was obviously thrilled at the thought of having a baby. This was something I had wanted my entire life. But there was a deeper resolution for me, too, in staring at that positive pregnancy test. After everything I had been through, after all the doctors' office visits, the medications to try and get a period and then to manage my bursting ovarian cysts, the hormonal imbalances, feeling like the "funny asexual friend" to every male I met, the breast deformities and complications, this was the first time I thought to myself, *Wow, I guess I really am a female. A woman.* It blew my mind in the most beautiful way.

I feel like I should pause here and say that I'm not making a sweeping statement about what it means to be a woman. I'm not suggesting that you aren't a "real" woman if you can't have children—not in the slightest. What I'm saying is that I recognized in that moment how much value and significance I had placed on this event to help me feel like my femininity was real. This, I presume, is why so many women experience deep grief when they're unable to conceive. It's about wanting to be a mother, sure. But it's also about wondering, *Am I really a woman? Is something wrong with me?*

These experiences leave their mark. They leave scars, whether we like it or not. We only get to decide what we want to do with those scars.

We can either look at the scars we bear on our hearts and our bodies as marks of imperfection, or we can find a way to celebrate those scars as tokens of healing, proof that we fought through something challenging and survived. I can't say I've done a perfect job of choosing the latter, but the longer I work at it, the more I realize it's the only path to peace and purpose and true healing.

If we're ever going to have a shot at reframing our scars as badges of honor rather than blemishes of shame, we have to do three things: we have to confront our fears; break free of our old, predictable patterns; and alter our perception of things so we can learn to see with new eyes. I'm getting there.

The day Brave entered the world, things didn't go as Colin and I had planned. It seems like birth rarely does.

I had a birth plan, which was, essentially, to labor as naturally as possible for as long as possible. I wanted to feel the pain of labor I'd been hearing about my whole life. If I'm honest, I think I figured it would make me feel more like a "real woman." Primal. But I told myself that if or when I literally could not take it anymore, I would do a walking epidural. The walking epidural is supposed to just take the edge off the pain as opposed to the full numbing that comes with a regular epidural.

Colin and I took birthing classes to learn how to properly breathe and adjust positions during labor. On top of the classes, I watched one too many documentaries on how mainstream doctors and hospitals often have an agenda and push women to labor the way they want them to (in their timeframe for schedule purposes and meeting numbers). So I decided to hire a doula to help support my birth plan. I felt prepared and ready to meet my baby boy.

But if you've never had a baby, nothing can fully prepare you for labor.

At 5 a.m., when I got up for one of my many middle-of-the-night pee breaks, my water broke all over our hardwood floor. It was the most interesting, otherworldly feeling. I ran back into the bedroom and told Colin, "It's happening, it's happening!" I got into the shower and sat on the floor as the water continued to come out, and I bawled my eyes out in wonder and anticipation that this was actually happening.

Contractions started, and I definitely felt the pain, but I thought to myself, "OK, I can handle this. I'm a woman. This is what I'm made for."

As the contractions got more painful, Colin and my doula coached me through how to breathe and what to do. But I threw everything out the window and just started screaming, "Ow! Ow! Ow! Ow! Ow! Ow! Ow!" over and over again. I was crying hysterically as we made our way to the hospital.

The drive was like a scene from a movie. I had a few heavy contractions as we drove over speed bumps. Each time we hit a bump, the pain seared, and I screamed at Colin in agony.

By the time we got to the hospital, I was 100 percent ready for a full epidural. I had experienced the pain and felt I'd earned my birth pain stripes, but now I needed a break. I couldn't handle it anymore. We pulled up to Cedars-Sinai hospital (where I was born) and—get ready for my little LA moment right here—nobody was available at valet parking. Yes, in LA, we valet even at the hospital.

So while we waited for a nurse with a wheelchair to come get me and someone to park the car, I had hoisted one leg up on the car's hood, screaming as people on the sidewalk walked by on the way to their brunch dates, staring. You will understand only if you, too, have experienced back labor—it turned out Brave was "sunny side up." I didn't find out until later that this was what was happening, but I learned both the hard way and via the doctor's explanation that this is one of the most painful types of labor because of how the baby is rubbing against the mother's spine while coming down the birth canal.

God bless women for bringing life into this world.

We finally made our way up to triage, which I thought would be a quick check-in process so I could get my drugs, but it took over an hour. Multiple nurses asked me the same questions over and over as they typed information into their computers.

"Ma'am, are you *sure* your water broke?"

"YES, I'M SURE! Now please get me the drugs."

When I was finally checked in, the anesthesiologist was tied up, so I didn't get the epidural for about another hour or so. Then, to my dismay, when they finally gave me the shot, it didn't actually kick in for another hour. So different from my expectation that once I reached the hospital, I'd get relief. It was hours and hours of feeling like a continuous bomb made up of knives and flames was exploding in my insides. Women who give birth naturally are my heroes. I do not understand that type of strength.

All I wanted to listen to during the entire twenty-four hours of labor was one of my favorite churchy worship albums, Hillsong United acoustic, on repeat. My husband was with me for the entire labor and delivery, and heard the songs over and over, too. He kept asking me if I wanted to change it for some variety, and each time I screamed, "NO! DON'T CHANGE IT!" He probably never wants to listen to that album ever again. Something about it was comforting, which was exactly what I needed. When you're in that amount of pain, sometimes you cling to what reminds you of the purest part of you, what comforts the deepest part of your soul.

One of the most terrifying parts of labor was when a nurse turned up Brave's heartbeat monitor, and it was clear his heart rate was slowing down. They pressed some alert buttons, and eight other nurses frantically ran in. They flipped me over on my hands and knees and hurriedly put an oxygen mask over my face to try to get Brave's heart rate back up. That happened about eight times. I was so scared.

Another thing that threw me off was that the doctor I'd been seeing all nine months of my pregnancy, who was supposed to deliver my baby, was out of town for a wedding when I went into labor. So she set me up with another doctor I'd never met before. This new doctor kept telling me she thought I needed to have a C-section because things were not progressing how they should. On top of that, I had the same blood clotting disorder my mom had. My mom hemorrhaged when she gave birth to me and almost died, so I was terrified to have a C-section.

Not to mention, I'm also allergic to every antibiotic I've ever taken. Whenever I've taken antibiotics, I not only get severe hives, but one time, after taking amoxicillin, I was driving on the freeway and went into anaphylactic shock. My throat started to close up. I called the doctor, and as I spoke, my voice started changing because my throat was closing. I looked in the mirror, and my entire face was covered in hives. The doctor told me to hang up and call 911. The fire department talked me through how to breathe through anaphylactic shock.

When they finally met me on the side of the freeway with an ambulance and fire trucks, they shot me up with fluids to help reduce the throat swelling so I could breathe. Then they rushed me to the hospital. I almost died that day from taking antibiotics, and all I could think as I was laboring was, *What if it happens again?*

You can see why I was afraid of having a C-section when they would need to give me an IV of antibiotics I'd never tried before.

It got to the point, after twenty-four hours of labor, where both my doctor and doula agreed that we needed to do a C-section and get the baby out safely. I backed down in defeat and concurred. They had to separate me from my husband temporarily, taking me to a different room to start the operation process. They lifted me onto a different bed and strapped my arms down wide like I was on a cross, so I couldn't move. It felt so inhumane and unnatural to be in that position. It was the most terrifying feeling I had ever felt. I was shaking, and my teeth were chattering uncontrollably. After they started numbing my abdomen, and I confirmed I couldn't feel the tests they started to do, they let Colin come in. He sat next to me and started bawling. I could tell he was scared, too. He later told me that he was praying and simultaneously saying his last goodbye to me at the same time. It was traumatic primarily because I wanted my baby to be delivered safely, but also because I genuinely didn't know what would happen to me or if my body could handle the medication combined with my blood clotting condition.

It felt like a lifetime, but in reality, it was probably thirty minutes of prep and thirty minutes for the actual surgery and stitching up. When I heard my baby boy cry, it was the happiest moment of my entire life. The doctors pulled Brave out, and I'll never forget their words: "Oh my God, what a giant baby!" Not only was he sunny side up, he was almost ten pounds.

Well, that explained that.

They put Brave on my chest. That moment—how can I describe it? It was hands-down the most incredible moment—and feeling—of my entire life. The highest high of all time. The love I felt was otherworldly. I've heard many women say this, but it's really something you cannot possibly grasp or explain until you're in that moment yourself.

We had already had the name Brave picked out months before. Both Colin and my doula later told me that as the doctor was cutting, the Bethel and Amanda Cook song, "You Make Me Brave," serendipitously happened to be playing, and as they pulled him out, the powerful bridge was climaxing as Amanda belts "You make me brave, you make me brave, you make me brave!" It seems as though that may have been a special kiss from heaven.

I know it sounds cliché to say the pain was worth it, but it was. It was worth it to hold my boy—my big, healthy baby boy.

For as long as I could remember, doctors had been trying to lower my expectations for what my body would (or rather wouldn't) be able to do. Sometimes that's been to my benefit, but constantly feeling like my body is broken, faulty, defective, and can't handle much has worn on me. But to lie there in that moment, holding my beautiful ten-pound baby boy, I realized my body had done it. I had done it. I was a woman and a mother and a hell of a strong one at that.

What a victory.

One thing few people talk about when it comes to giving birth is the postpartum recovery. I was not prepared for it at all. I honestly screamed just as loud as I did during labor for much of the following days. The surgery scars burned and throbbed. The flaming, stabbing pain coming from the inside out was even worse than labor, so I was back to screaming for more drugs.

The body is a magnificent thing, and eventually healing came, but it was a process.

Right on track, doctors told me they weren't sure I'd be able to breastfeed because of all the breast issues. But I still wanted to try. I met with a lactation consultant after delivery and started the journey. A lot of women complain and say no one ever tells them what a challenge breastfeeding can be. It's true. It's a lot harder and more complicated than I was expecting. It's like an art to learn the rules, the grip, and the angles you need to perfect to get the baby to latch and the milk to come out. It's really a learning curve.

To my amazement, I had some success. (Don't you love when life never turning out how you expect actually works in your favor?) After some trial and error, I breastfed Brave for *nine months* until . . . drum roll . . .

One day I noticed a red lump on my left breast near where it was hard. The hardness was still my "normal" from all those years ago, so I didn't think much of it. Then the red spot started to hurt. I realized it was really bothering me when I laid on my chest during yoga. Then, when I got home and looked in the mirror, I realized it was getting bigger and more red.

Naturally, I went to Google, which immediately revealed to me that I was dying of a terminal illness and might as well call it quits right then and there. My slightly hypochondriac self was *convinced* I had breast cancer. I stayed up all night planning the end of my life and my last goodbyes, pondering my life story and existence. Then I did the only next logical thing I could think of to do: I called Cedars-Sinai breast cancer center and made an appointment.

The doctor evaluated the situation and did some testing. I found out I had a common infection, called mastitis, that many women get when breastfeeding. My first response? Relief. *An infection is way better than breast cancer,* I told myself. But the doctor also said it was really bad, and I needed to start taking antibiotics. There was my old friend *panic* again.

The doctor instructed me to send her pictures throughout the week so she could track the progression of the infection.

Unfortunately, a week later, I was back at the doctor's office because, even with the antibiotics, the infection had gotten ten times worse.

I went from the highest of highs, finally feeling like a woman for the first time in my life, back to feeling like a sickly, faulty-bodied girl. My doctor did an ultrasound, and when she told me the results, I couldn't believe was happening. She said the mastitis had now infected the breast implant, which can be deadly. It was eating through my skin and had to be removed within twenty-four hours. The doctor said to be careful hugging people and sleeping that night, because the implant was about to come through my skin.

THROUGH MY SKIN.

Now, to remind you, my previous three breast surgeries had been so traumatic that after the last one went terribly, I left the breast implant in my body, *scarred and hard, for seventeen years.* I just couldn't bring myself to undergo a fourth surgery and risk the trauma of more complications. So I left it. I tried to block out the scar-tissued hard boob and kept kicking the can further away in denial. Now, after seventeen years, my efforts to ignore my body had brought me to this very inconvenient place. I had no choice but to deal with it.

Life has a way of not letting us run away from our giants.

It knows we have another fight in us to get to deeper healing.

To say I didn't want to have to go through another traumatic surgery is a major understatement, but I didn't have time to debate about it or keep shelving the issue. This thing had to get removed.

I called Colin to tell him the news, and we made arrangements for me to have surgery the next day. It was clear what needed to happen, but I still had another decision to make. The doctor told me that after the breast implant was removed, it had to be left out for at least six to eight months. In my previous surgeries, they'd replaced the implant in the same surgery. But not this time. It was too risky. As scared as I was, I knew I had to face my fear. I didn't have a choice. This infection was bad, and foregoing surgery wasn't an option.

Here's the catch. Because I was currently breastfeeding, my breasts were double their normal size (one of my personal favorite perks of breastfeeding, which made me feel extra woman-like, feminine, and—dare I say—sexy for the first time in my life). So when they removed the one implant, I'd have two *very* different size boobs. The thought of cutting one off and having one huge boob and one totally flat, quadruple-scarred, cut-off boob sent me into a mental tailspin.

Not only was I just getting the hang of breastfeeding and so happy it was working, but now I'd be worse off than before my original surgery. Like any woman, I just wanted two breasts around the same size.

I didn't have much time to process this. I had to make a decision. So I decided to remove the implant in the other breast as well and just start from an equal playing field of scarred-up flatness on both sides.

Thankfully, I made it through the surgery itself without a glitch. But of course, then I had to face the dreaded moment when the bandage would be removed. Then I would see what my chopped-up chest looked like. Fair warning: I'm going to describe this to you because I am tired of hiding, and I want you to get the full picture of how far healing can take us. I want you to know the kind of scars I'm wearing (and have since learned to wear as badges of honor), so that you can do the same with yours. No scar is too ugly or too deep to be your symbol of courage, resilience, femininity, and grace.

But, at the time, when I saw my chest, I literally gasped out loud. I'd seen my boobs look like a lot of things in my life, but this was the worst yet.

Because the infection had eaten away at my skin, they had to cut off my skin—the whole bottom of my left breast. Now my left side was even more deformed. Both of my boobs were now not only completely flat and covered in scars, but the left nipple was now pulled down, creating a hook-like shape.

When I showed one of my best girlfriends, I warned her first and said my left boob looked kind of like a rat face. A downward-facing rat face.

When she saw it, she looked at it and said, "Actually, I think it looks more like a downward-facing wiener dog face."

She was right. Spot-on. Talk about sexy, right?

I know I should have simply been thankful to be alive. I should have been thankful for a husband who loves me and a happy, healthy baby and friends I can laugh with and on and on. And I am thankful for those things. At the same time, I want to be honest about how challenging it's been to make peace with my own scars, so that you don't get discouraged when the time comes to make peace with yours.

About a week after my surgery, I went in for a post-op checkup. When the doctor opened my gown, her jaw dropped, and she let out an expletive I was surprised to hear a professional doctor say. The look on her face said it all—she didn't have to actually *say* anything. I knew it was worse than she had expected. My heart sank. Instant trigger of a lifetime of past trauma of doctors' reactions at seeing my chest.

My breasts now looked so drastically abnormal and deformed, even the *doctor* didn't know what to do. Would there be any coming back from this? Would I ever feel like a woman again?

Since I had to wait six to eight months before getting any reconstruction done, to let my body recover from the infection and surgery,

I blocked out how ugly I felt—and didn't look at my chest—in order to keep up with my life. I dove into work and being a mom. I hustled to make sure people were getting their paychecks. I continued to put out fires at work. I took care of my toddler. I tried my best to be a loving wife, while my attention also shifted significantly to parenting. I didn't really process everything I had just gone through as much as I should have.

It was still too painful to give the issue the love, care, and emotional healing it needed.

The six-to eight-month window I had to wait to do reconstructive surgery came and went. I thought that during that time period, I'd have some profound revelation and start loving my body again. That I'd embrace my new deformation. Be empowered. Somehow be more confident. But I didn't.

Colin was so sweet to say he loved me no matter what, and that he even liked the new "sporty/athletic" look for me now. I appreciated him looking on the bright side. But I still had a lot of work to do to believe in myself again.

Even when I knew I could safely have surgery to try to "fix" my body again, my inner Peace-o-Meter kept saying I needed to wait. Deep down, I knew there was some deeper healing that needed to happen, and I felt like that needed to happen while I was feeling deformed—before I had any type of surgery again, if ever. I wanted to sit with the pain. Sit with the deformity. I wanted to finally learn to truly *love my flaws* as I had been instructing so many other young women to do.

I knew that, in order to do this, I had to go to the depths before I could come out on the other side. After all, this has been a lifelong struggle. I felt that if I were to have another reconstructive surgery before I did the hard work of healing what was beneath the scars, it would just be a Band-Aid. So I put off the surgery. I knew surgery only had the power to "fix" my outside. But more than that, I knew I needed to invest in healing on the inside.

Have you ever realized a flaw or an area in your life you know needs to heal or improve, but don't know how to get to the other side? I think the hardest part is realizing you feel hopeless that healing could ever come. You have a problem. You need to grow. But of course you don't know how. So you find yourself wondering what to do next.

At the time, I was going to "Mommy & Me" classes where a child development specialist taught us about different topics. On one particular day, the topic was learning how to wean your baby off breastfeeding in the healthiest way. I learned it's usually a three-to six-month process. At first, I started to check out because I had already stopped breastfeeding Brave. But I started to listen when other mothers started crying as they talked about how difficult it was for them—how emotional it was for them to have to stop breastfeeding, how difficult it was for the baby, and how much they would both miss it. I sat there thinking to myself, "Wow, I didn't get time to grieve any of that." I just powered through because I had no choice.

When I found out about the infection, I had to stop breastfeeding immediately. No weaning process, just cold turkey. And until that moment, I hadn't realized I needed to allow myself to grieve. I had done what I had to do, but as I sat in that meeting, it dawned on me how I'd had *tunnel vision* about the breast infection and surgery, about work and mom life. I hadn't taken time to cope with or grieve what happened to my body in a healthy way, let alone grieving having to stop breastfeeding or thinking about what that experience was like for Brave.

So right then and there, as I listened to those other women, I began to let myself grieve. I let myself be sad, think about what had happened, and begin to accept it.

Then, the most amazing thing happened to me. I experienced grace for myself. Normally, this would have been a realization I'd beat myself up about. But I didn't. I was able to let the emotions and reflections on the last year of my life pass over me in waves. I was able to grieve, process, and accept them. I couldn't control what happened to me, but I had a choice to make. I could allow shame to take over or embrace the struggle and look at it all as another opportunity to grow.

Sometimes—*most* of the time—our stories don't fit perfectly within the guidelines of "how everything is supposed to be." Even when we experience real challenges and struggles, we always have a choice about our attitude. We can be victims of our circumstances and choose to feel negative about the cards we're dealt. Or, we can take our afflictions and choose to see them from an end game perspective: as ultimately positive because they give us a fighting chance to reach our fullest, most beautiful potential.

For the first time in my life—after years of despising my body and ignoring the pain my breasts have caused me—I chose to look at my situation as a new narrative, the narrative that this is another opportunity for me to grow. It's part of my unique story. It's part of my journey.

Later that night, I pulled out my journal and wrote in big, bold letters: MY NEW SCARS MAKE ME A UNIQUE, POWERFUL WARRIOR FILLED WITH NEW DEPTH AND INSPIRATION.

This now hangs on my bedroom wall. It is my new story. My new narrative. I want it to be yours, too.

Your scars tell the story of something beautiful: the story of you as a fighter, the story of your healing, the story of your resilience.

chapter ten

IMPERFECT IS THE NEW PERFECT

> If you have forgiven yourself for being imperfect
> and falling, you can now do it for just about
> everyone else. If you have not done it for yourself,
> I'm afraid you will likely pass on your sadness,
> absurdity, and judgment and futility to others.
> —Richard Rohr

Parenting a toddler gives you firework highs—the first steps and the angel-soft skin and the magical heart-melting moments when they tell you they love you forever. Then the high wears off, and you hit the lows, when the temper tantrums flare up and your child turns into a terrorist version of himself who is out to destroy you.

There's nothing quite so delightful and heartwarming as your child screaming bloody murder as if you were *abducting* him when you're simply trying to change his diaper, feed him, or hold his hand to cross the street so he doesn't get hit by a car.

Before being a mom, I never felt such deep love. I'd never trade it. Also, before I was a mom, I never felt like I was being held hostage by a tiny terrorist. I never considered I'd bribe my child with french fries and videos just to get him into a car seat. Never dreamed how crazy-making it would be to have someone scream "no" "don't talk" and "go away" at you three hundred times in a row. When I can't get him to stop biting, hitting, screaming, or throwing the dog bone at my face, it makes me feel like the least sane version of myself. Like I'm going to spontaneously combust or, at the very least, like I want to punch a hole in the wall.

And sleep deprivation is real, people. It. Is. Real. It makes all of the above feel like you're drowning with no light at the end of the tunnel.

People always told me parenting is simultaneously the best and hardest thing they've done. And it's true. Of course, I had days before being a mother when I felt like a failure. Now there are just more of them—and the stakes are higher. When you mess up at work, at least you get to go home to your safe haven. Having any kind of peaceful, serene, restful haven with a toddler at home is impossible. Then there's the tiny issue of being responsible for keeping a human being alive.

I can't think of an area of my life where I want to fail less or an area where I am more prone to fail. Maybe this is what makes parenting so terrifying: it makes us vulnerable. It's a reminder of something that's true in all of life: failure is inevitable. Our failure may hurt those we love. Still, somehow, there is an inexplicable grace that comes like a warm blanket and covers us all.

For example, my friend Megan and I embrace the grace by taking pictures of how long our leg hair is and sending them to each other. It helps us to know (and see) that we aren't alone in our exhaustion and self-care imperfection. Sometimes I even show

Colin pics of her leg hair so he knows I'm "normal." I can't say how long we've been doing this, but I can tell you that it's a deeply cathartic exercise, one I recommend wholeheartedly. You may think I'm crazy, but that's just because you haven't tried it. Give it a shot. Go ahead. It's easy. Simply take a picture of your hairy legs (you know they're hairy right now) and send it to an unsuspecting friend of yours. Say Caitlin Crosby told you to do it. You will not regret this, I promise.

Some days I wake up to Brave jumping in bed with me and smile to myself, thinking, this is the *best* way to start my day. Then his razor-sharp toenail, which I neglected to clip, slices open my thigh. Blood starts gushing down my leg, and next thing I know, my sheets look like a murder scene.

Some days I'm trying to remember to take care of fifty important to-do's, and I forget to eat. On those days, I usually don't have time to go buy food between meetings. So naturally, I do what any resourceful person would do. I devour Brave's baby food pouches. (Which might not be so bad if I didn't also find myself reaching back to grab his old goldfish crackers from deep in the cracks of his car seat. I wish I was kidding.)

I've shown up to work with old, dried fermented milk throw-up on my face (and clothes and shoes). I have milk splotches on my black Kenneth Cole leather jacket that are two years old. I think it makes it look more original and artsy, like I'm a cool painter or something.

And then, of course, there was the time I made up my mind to have a positive attitude and look for all the small things throughout the day to be grateful for. No matter what happened. Of course, the first day of this little experiment, I woke up at 4 a.m. to a screaming baby and tried unsuccessfully to change his diaper—an ordeal that ended with poop in his hair, under my fingernails, and on our walls—while I was simultaneously dreading a pretty serious fire I had to put out at work that day. By the time I finished cleaning up the mess, Brave had thrown multiple sharp objects at my face, so I woke up Colin and handed Brave to him, saying, "I can't *take* this anymore!" Then I raced to the other room, dropped to my knees, and started crying.

This was all before 7 a.m.

A few minutes later, as I sat on the couch feeling defeated, Brave poked his head around the corner. He came up to me, holding his Thomas the Train toy, and reached out to give me a hug. It was sweet and soothing—exactly what I needed. But I didn't realize his electronic train was turned on. The next thing I knew, my hair was caught in its wheels, and I could not seem to shut the toy off. After struggling for thirty minutes to detach myself, I pulled out the scissors. Let's just say I went to work that day with a unique new look.

We aspire to be "perfect," but if we're honest, perfect isn't relatable, and because it's not relatable, it's often not very likable. Perfect is intimidating. It can bring out the worst in us: envy, compassion, fear of not being enough. In this way, perfect alienates us all. But when someone is brave enough to show us their imperfections, we have an immediate connection. We're able to relax and be at peace together in our humanity. We *like* imperfect people because they're just like us. And they give us permission to be imperfect, just as we are. Imperfection brings us together.

Social media has a way of isolating us, breaking that human connection and adding to the pressure to uphold a standard of perfection. Social media paints the picture that we have it all together as we are; that we are happy, successful and #blessed. But the reality is that life is hard, the world and political climate are chaotic, people we love get sick, and we lose people we love deeply. Scars form. Hardship and pain are inevitable. So how do we stay engaged? How do we jump in and enjoy every single second of this colorful life? I won't always get it right, but I'm going to keep trying until it becomes easier and easier, and eventually, I hope, it will be second nature.

According to researchers,

> The pull of social media addiction isn't all in our heads. It's quite real, thanks to two chemicals our brains produce: dopamine and oxytocin . . . Dopamine is stimulated by unpredictability, by small bits of information, and by reward cues—pretty much the exact conditions of social media. The pull of dopamine is so strong that studies have shown tweeting is harder for people to resist than cigarettes and alcohol. Then there's oxytocin, sometimes referred to as 'the cuddle chemical' because it's released when you kiss or hug. Or . . . tweet. In 10 minutes of social media time, oxytocin levels can rise as much as 13%—a hormonal spike equivalent to some people on their wedding day. And all the goodwill that comes with oxytocin—lowered stress levels, feelings of love, trust, empathy, generosity—comes with social media, too.[*]

The point is, our brains are chemically wired to become addicted to social media. So it's no wonder we're scrolling for hours, trapped in comparison, and presenting only the "best" versions of ourselves to get that high.

I've been just as addicted to social media as the next person. Those little "likes" and nice comments really do numb me away from reality in the moment, but I know it's a trap to get caught up in it. I post plenty of happy, pretty moments from my life on there

---

[*] Courtney Seiter, "The Psychology of Social Media: Why We Like, Comment, and Share Online," Buffer, https://buffer.com/resources/psychology-of-social-media.

(that's not bad to do, by the way), but I love balancing them out with real, vulnerable posts to make the whole social media world seem less toxic. To show the full story.

If you want proof that we crave real human connection online, I got the highest number of "likes" on my *most* unfiltered Instagram post, a post I tried to talk myself out of because it felt too vulnerable. Yes, this elevated my oxytocin levels, but I also believe and hope it gave permission to people to be real and know they aren't alone when life is hard.

You can find the post if you want to see it. It's a split screen with two pictures of my face. On the left, my face is red from crying really hard, and I have mascara running down my face. In the picture on the right, I'm fully decked out in makeup and looking presentable. Here's what I shared on Instagram:

I hesitated posting this, but I think it's important. We see people on social media & think their filtered lives look "perfect." We maybe assume they're happy and "have it all." I know it's "normal" for social media to be the "best of" our lives, but I think sharing REAL LIFE and vulnerability might be a better use of this thing. The pic on the left was taken Friday at 6 p.m. The pic on the right was taken an hour later at 7 p.m during date night. Makeup, filter and all. The pic on the left FAR better describes real life on the inside. Going through difficult, gut-wrenching family stuff; feeling stressed, overwhelmed, disappointed, brain dead, like a "not good enough" mom, boss, wife, daughter, friend, CEO, woman; and just beyond beyond beyond exhausted. But I don't normally post those real feelings on here. I post the inspiring TEDx Talk moments, the Oprah moments, and all the lives that are being changed at @thegivingkeys moments. (Which I'm SO honored to be a part of!) I post how cute my baby is when he's laughing, but no one sees the screaming tantrums, hitting, and constant #momfails. People are so proud and impressed that we are opening our first retail store and just had our @thegivingkeys 10-year anniversary (which IS amazing and so exciting!) but don't know the sacrifices, stress, sleepless nights, and trauma behind everything. I will still continue to post the special and beautiful moments in life, because those are real, too; I just don't want people to feel alone in the struggle of depression, insecurity, and ALL the complicated things that make us human. Here's a reminder to not compare yourself to anyone on social media! It's not real!!! #yourenotalone

We're all failing at something. No one can possibly hold up all elements of their life—job, family, friends, rest, self-care, fitness, education—to the level of perfection we somehow try to attain. It's not only impossible, it's unnecessary. We're all imperfect, and this is what makes us human.

I wrote this song called, "Imperfect is the New Perfect," for my first album and still love to jam out (in 2008 pop-rock style) to it:

Compare the way my body
Looks to the magazines
Don't know why everybody's
Buying into the scene

I don't wanna look like you because you're
Too perfect, too perfect
And I don't wanna fill your shoes because it's
Not worth it, not worth it

Just dry your eyes, you're beautiful
I understand, it's logical
'Cause these images are everywhere
They're make-believe, so don't compare

We're every shape and size, you know we're
Just perfect, we're just perfect
We love our hips, our thighs, because they're
Just perfect, just perfect

I don't fit the mold, I am real
Too colorful to conceal
Imperfect is the new perfect

Last year we created a new campaign for The Giving Keys jewelry—the I AM collection. Each piece included a set of two keys. One key said I AM and the other had various words such as BRAVE, FEARLESS, STRONG, and LOVED. During the campaign, our marketing director asked what word I wanted. I suddenly felt embarrassed to say that I wanted I AM STRONG. She said, "Oh, that's perfect for you because you ARE so strong!" And I said, "Nooooooo. No way. I actually want to get that word because I feel the opposite. I feel so weak."

In that moment, I realized I'd been living small. That's what the pressure of perfectionism can do to us. I hadn't been walking in the truth that I *am* strong.

Just because I didn't naturally feel strong didn't mean it wasn't true. But I needed to change the narrative I was telling myself. Sometimes you have to stop and catch yourself. So I made myself write out a list of all the things that prove I am strong. I needed to reprogram myself—out with the negative self-talk, in with the positive self-talk. It was time to walk tall in my strength. I needed to believe it. I needed to champion myself. To kick off the pressure to not fail.

So I got my I AM STRONG necklace and wore it as a reminder, as a tool to help me *own* my strength.

I needed that necklace because it speaks to something deeply important: *We become what we believe.* So start practicing believing you are strong, brave, fearless, and loved. Train yourself to believe the best about yourself, and that's exactly what you will become.

I was recently invited to a high-profile fashion show. I've been to a few fashion shows in my day, but that was before I was pregnant or had kids. In the past, when I was an "artist," I had a record label, PR company, and a stylist they hired to help get me ready. The stylist would help pick an appropriate outfit, and all my hair and makeup would be scheduled and done. Yes, a "glam squad" as they call it. A seat was reserved for me, and I'd just show up and enjoy the event.

However, this time was different from the start because I was pregnant with my second child, my daughter, Love. I was also maxed from running a company full time and taking care of my toddler, so I didn't prioritize preparing for the event. Plus, I no longer had the "glam squad" to assist me. One of the challenges was finding something appropriate and flattering to wear. Maternity clothes are typically not high-fashion (surprise surprise), so I rampaged through my closet, trying to make something work. I ended up wearing pants that were *not* maternity pants and only zipped them up halfway. I wore a shirt jacket long enough to cover the fact that my pants weren't zipped up and my butt crack was hanging out the back. It was the same pantsuit my designer friend made and which I wore

during my second TEDx Talk, "Backwards Business Plan," as well as
to countless other photo shoots and important events.

It was faux pas enough to wear the same clothes multiple times
to public events, but even worse, they were dirty because I hadn't
cleaned them after the last few times I wore them. At this point,
though, I had run out of time and didn't have any other options.

I thought I had shoes that would work well enough, but when
I tried them at the last minute, I realized all the shoes I'd thought
would work were worn down to the point that there was no rub-
ber bottom on at least one of the heels. When I walked, I not only
walked with an uneven limp from one heel being higher than the
other, but also made a sound like nails on a chalkboard. Classy.

It was an hour before the show, and I had to find a new pair of
shoes stat. I raced off to the fastest and closest shoe place I could
think of. There's a Marshalls around the block, so I found myself
buying a clearance, two-seasons-ago pair of Nine West heels for
$15.99. They were size 11 (which was too big for me) but beggars
can't be choosers. I bought the shoes and rushed back home to
get ready.

I was feeling a bit insecure with my pieced-together outfit,
knowing I'd show up at this high-profile fashion show surrounded
by gorgeously groomed women, A-list celebrities, and creative
designers. But just as I was heading out the door, my sweet husband
said something I really needed to hear: "Just remember, all the glitz
and the glam and the models might look amazing, like they have
it all, but they probably want what you have. And all you need is
here with Brave and me and our family. That's what really matters."

As I pulled up to that fashion show with my dirty, half-zipped
pants, unshaven legs, makeup I'd applied en route, tweezing my
chin hairs in my visor mirror as I pulled up to valet (yes, it's true),
and wearing too-big marked-down Marshalls heels (with paper

towels stuffed in the toes to keep them on), I carried Colin's words with me. I walked in with confidence and pride, knowing that those shoes were holding up a pregnant woman with hairy legs who was doing her best for herself and her family.

In that moment, I felt like my own real-life superhero.

Caring for one human being and growing another while juggling everything else in my life is about as strong and badass as it comes. It didn't matter what anyone else thought of me that day. I knew all my imperfections were *my* perfect.

Let's do more of this for ourselves. For our partners. For our kids. For our families. Let's see it as endearing. Let's see it as creative. Let's see it as our brilliance. Let's see it as our genius. Let's see it as beauty. Let's give ourselves a break and let ourselves be human.

Let's lead with our own imperfect and give others the gift of offering more grace to themselves.

With all your so-called mess-ups and low moments, my question to you is this: Can you let your imperfections *be*, and let that be perfect enough?

chapter eleven

LET YOURSELF FAIL

When we fail, we are merely joining the great parade of humanity that has walked ahead of us, and will follow after us.
—Richard Rohr

At times, I have felt like I was unraveling. I was drowning in the responsibilities of being a CEO, a mother, a wife, a daughter, a friend. How was I supposed to keep up? How were other people keeping up?

Other times, I would look around my life and think, *I have a loving husband, a healthy baby boy, a thriving business, a life full of people who love me. How is it possible to feel empty, depressed, anxiety-ridden, and like a failure in the midst of all the good?* The tension between the sky-high expectations that seemed to weigh heavy on me and the deeper understanding that I already had everything I needed continually plagued me.

We bought our house from a professional woman who is married and has two toddlers. She seemed healthy, poised, and confident—like she was successfully holding her life together. I only met her twice, but from the outside, she didn't seem like a basket case, which was a win in my book.

"How do you do it?" I asked her one day when she was picking up her mail on the way to work.

"I started with knowing that in order to keep my priorities my priorities, I'd have to let other areas go," she said. "Other than working full-time to provide for my family and spending time taking care of my kids, I don't do much else. I don't see my mother much. She probably thinks I'm the worst daughter. I don't have time to be there for my friends right now. They probably think I'm the worst friend. There are only so many hours in a day, and I have to decide how I want to use them."

It struck me because she said it so matter-of-factly, without caveats or a self-deprecating tone of voice. She fully owned where she was at in life. It inspired me. It was obvious she'd stopped beating herself up about what she was letting go of. She accepted her life, which seemed to be giving her a lot of freedom.

I decided to take her advice. I came up with my own mantra: "Every day, let yourself fail at something." Failing intentionally was a reminder to myself that failure is inevitable. It was also a way to normalize that it's OK to never find that elusive "perfect balance." Maybe, I thought, after a few months of this practice, failure wouldn't even feel much like "failure" anymore. Maybe it would actually feel like health—healthy boundaries and healthy decisions.

The first morning I put my plan to intentionally fail into practice, I forced myself to get out the door and go to a yoga class, as I knew my body needed some tending to.

To give you a bit of context, for months, I'd made it a priority to spend time with Brave in the morning, at the expense of taking care of myself and my body. As a result, my hormones were out of whack, my energy was low, and I was still struggling to feel like myself again. On this particular day, my plan was to sacrifice the time I'd usually spend with Brave in the morning before work, in order to take care of myself—*big for me*. A way to "fail" at something but also to succeed at something else, I supposed. The plan was, I'd come home, shower, get ready, and head to work.

But when I got home from yoga, Brave took hold of my leg with a death grip, and I could tell he needed me. In that moment, I knew I couldn't spend time with Brave, get showered and ready, and *also* make it to work on time. So I made a decision. I decided what I was going to fail at. I owned it. I just plopped onto the floor in my sweaty yoga clothes and sat with Brave. We snuggled and played, and I forfeited my shower and getting ready. I drove to work that day in damp, smelly workout clothes, with unbrushed teeth, greasy hair, and the biggest smile on my face.

In the past, I 100 percent would have been shaming myself and feeling disgusting on my way to work. Instead, I felt free because I'd shifted my perspective. I had *chosen* what to fail at. Instead of lamenting that I had lost control and couldn't handle all of the day's demands, I decided what was most important and freed myself to fail at the rest. I acknowledged I couldn't do it all. And in return, I smiled with confidence, knowing I had done what was most important that day.

There's freedom in giving yourself permission to fail, and to choose what you're going to fail at. We're humans, not robots. We're not supposed to "do it all." Life isn't a show. What an incredible experience it is to be human, have limitations, and be able to choose what is most important to us, even in the smallest moments.

For example, maybe you have to choose between:

- a healthy, home-cooked breakfast and turning in a project on time
- being present to visiting in-laws or cleaning the bathroom sink as they're coming in the front door
- taking the night to answer all of your unread emails or go on a stress-relieving walk outside

~

It's one thing to fail at showering for a day and quite another to fail at something like a marriage, your job, or showing up for a family member who is sick and needs help. So what happens when we have to fail at the things that really matter to us?

One day, during my "fail on purpose" season, Colin and I were sitting on the couch. It had been a full day, as usual. I'd been rushing from meeting to meeting all day, trying to make sure everyone had what they needed, and now I just needed a moment to decompress on the couch. But before I could fully settle into the moment, Colin looked at me and said, "Caitlin, The Giving Keys has eaten you alive." I could see the mixture of his frustration, compassion, and grief. It was coming from a place of love and concern for me, for us.

Cue *tears*. When your husband looks you in the eye and expresses how your work has taken a toll on you and your marriage, it's a terrible feeling. I couldn't deny it. I knew it was true. I felt it, too. I just didn't know what to do about it. I was exhausted trying to do it all but felt trapped. I felt like I needed to keep working hard not only to provide for my family, but also help keep an entire staff employed so they could provide for their families. No pressure.

When you think you can't take one more thing, there's always one more thing.

Stress made anxiety my constant companion. I was fighting it as best as I could, but I wasn't succeeding. When it came to choosing what to fail at, I didn't know what to do. I knew I had to make some major shifts and get help.

I began to think it might be best to try anti-anxiety medication for the first time, but I didn't want to without trying other options first. I didn't want to numb myself in order to cope with my life. Still, I wasn't sure what options I had left.

I went to a holistic doctor, who prescribed me a more natural low dose of anti-anxiety medication, but I didn't really feel much different. I had fewer heart pains, so that was a plus. But ultimately, I decided to stop the medication and try to cope with the anxiety naturally—that's what felt right for me and my body—so I went back to the same holistic doctor to see what other options there might be. The doctor explained to me the power and science behind taking deep breaths to calm the nervous system. In fact, she suggested I try a simple exercise and see how it worked for me. Here's how to do it:

Inhale deeply for a count of three. During that deep inhalation, mentally identify something that's causing you stress. When you get to the top of the inhale, hold the breath and the stressor for a count of three. While you do this, tell yourself there will be a solution for the stressful situation or thought. Then exhale for a count of three, releasing the breath and mentally releasing the stressor. Let it go. Repeat this exercise cycle as many times as you need to for the one particular stress point. Repeat the breath work until you start to feel peace that there *will* be a solution.

Imagine me, locked in the bathroom stall at work for an abnormally long time, repeating this exercise before a staff meeting. Everyone's wondering, "What's going on with Caitlin in there? What are those noises?"

One thing I found to be interesting about this approach—which was effective for me on many occasions—was that the solution doesn't have to be identified. The goal is that you gain peace that you or your higher power will find a resolution. You then repeat the exercise for any other stressful or challenging situations that are causing you anxiety, until you start to feel peace about those, too.

The science behind deep breathing and stress relief is compelling, and in my experience, it works. I've continued to use this simple technique when I catch my heart rate increasing and feel anxiety sweeping over me. When you battle anxiety, you don't question what works. You just do it. This may sound a little woo-woo, but rubbing some lavender essential oil into your hands to breathe in deeply makes the experience even more complete—and leaves the office bathroom smelling nice for the next person.

Always pay it forward.

When I was pregnant with Love, I started going to prenatal yoga classes with Rebecca Benenati. She's an experienced yoga instructor, doula, and women's health expert in LA. Rebecca has such a peaceful, secure, wise, confidence about her, and I wanted that to rub off on me.

One day, after her class, I felt led to ask her advice. I shared with her my thoughts on there being a societal issue with how, as women, we are "trained" to see our bodies a certain way. I've always felt, since my LoveYourFlawz days, that the media and entertainment industry is brainwashing everyone with toxic, unrealistic, and twisted expectations. I knew she'd been part of over 100 births and helped thousands of women through the transition of changing bodies, so I wanted to know: What did she see from her side of the story? Especially when it comes to breasts, did other women struggle with the experience and aftermath of their metamorphosis? If so, what was the solution? What did she see after working with other women? If she could give me any advice about body image, especially postpartum, what would it be?

I'll be forever grateful for what took place over the next hour.

Rebecca shared some of her own experiences and how the body reflects how we feel about ourselves. She said, "As women, we are often short on confidence, and it's really sad because we are *so* powerful." She told me there needs to be an element of making peace with our bodies that must take place before we can begin to carry ourselves with the confidence that is our birthright.

I opened up a little bit about what I'd been through—the health issues, breast surgeries, and so on. Rebecca looked at me with gentleness and care. She told me that after years of working with people and their bodies, she can see where people hold their wounds.

She said, "Now I know why your shoulders fold forward. Your shoulders round forward to protect your breasts—your heart."

Without knowing what the specific issue was, Rebecca said, she would have guessed my wound had something to do with my heart center.

"But now I see it truly *is* an issue connected to your heart," she said. "The pain is related to your breasts—a part of your body that you're learning to accept, love, be kind to, and respect. It's all coming from your heart."

I took a deep breath. I couldn't even begin to explain how true this felt. It felt true beyond what my mind could understand. It felt true down to the very core of who I was.

"[Regarding] the inner work you've been doing around this particular part of your body, I'd venture to suggest there is some shame connected to what's going on," Rebecca said.

I nodded. "I want to heal."

"Of course you do. Can we try something?"

Rebecca led me through several exercises. She said we needed to open up my back and shoulders to physically bring a sense of confidence to my body. She had me stand up and retract my shoulders, hold myself confidently—as if confidence was the feeling running through my whole body. She instructed me to use my breath from the inside to bring fullness into my chest. To energetically breathe fullness into my breasts. To breathe in that I'm perfect just the way I am.

She also said it could be helpful to move the energy in my body to assist in my healing related to my breast trauma.

"Move the energy through my body?" I asked. "How would I do that?"

"*Reiki* is a Japanese word, but it's essentially a stress-reduction practice where the practitioner lays hands on or above an area of a person's body that needs healing," Rebecca explained.

I had heard of Reiki before, but had been cautious in my younger years because I worried that the practice might be incongruent with my faith. But after Rebecca explained it to me, it struck me how similar it was to the Christian tradition of praying over people with your hands. This was something that actually felt very familiar to me because I've used my hands to pray over people many times before. When you think about it, it's such a beautiful thing for human beings to lend our support to one other—physically, emotionally, and spiritually—by laying hands on someone in pain or struggle.

"Do you want to try a little bit of it?" Rebecca asked.

I nodded.

Just like that, our little chat turned into this impromptu, rather intimate session of her walking me through exercises, laying her hands on my body. While she did it, I felt peace for miles.

As I lay there on my back, trying to allow more peace and energy to move in my body, you could hear the "thump, thump" of Beyoncé's "Who Run the World (Girls)" coming from another workout class in the room next door. Rebecca and I both laughed. On one hand, *how appropriate.* On the other hand, "Who Run the World (Girls)" isn't really the Reiki healing vibe. So Rebecca put on classical, instrumental yoga music in our room. As I lay on my back, she just placed her hands on my left shoulder and my left chest area.

As I lay there, simultaneously hearing peaceful yoga music and Beyoncé, I couldn't help but smile to myself. I loved the juxtaposition of the two completely opposite types of music playing while Rebecca's hands were on me, supporting my healing. Rebecca was creating this calm, healing moment for me; and in tandem, Beyoncé was reminding me that, as a woman, I really do have the power to create life, the strength to be a boss, and the fierce, matchless feminine intuition to care for people well. I have it in me to run the world—or, at the very least, my world.

I closed my eyes and allowed the experience to soak in. As I did, I realized I could be free from the shame I'd carried about my body for so long. The shame I'd carried about not keeping up and trying to be successful at everything in my life. The shame about "messing up" in marriage, "messing up" as a mother, "messing up" as a boss, "messing up" as an actress and singer, "messing up" as a daughter. There was so much grace. There was grace enough for all of it.

As I lay on that yoga room floor, I realized I could have grace for myself. This was part of the healing I needed. I needed to give myself the very grace I was so bent on extending to others.

None of us were meant to go through life carrying a truckload of shame on our backs. Shame is one of the most debilitating and crippling weights to carry. We will all take our own path through this life. No matter what your path is, I'm certain you'll make some wrong turns, you'll wonder if you're getting it "right," you'll question yourself and question the people around you. But I deeply believe you have it within you to embrace and release the pain you've withstood. Whatever it is about—something physical, heartbreak, addiction, broken dreams, an earlier trauma—don't stop seeking healing. Perhaps the failure, the wound, the pain, or the longing was allowed or placed there for a reason. To stretch you. To remind you that you have a fighter inside you. Don't ever quit believing you can heal. And while healing and being restored to wholeness doesn't mean you'll then be spotless, perfect, and unmarred, healing and restoration is there for you. Freedom is there for you. Your own kind of restoration. Your own kind of freedom. Your own kind of masterpiece.

Give yourself grace on your journey of failing and healing because you're enough right now, just as you are.

My old song, "Flawz" reminds me of this:

My skin isn't clear, Haven't spoke in a year
Cuz I still have fear I'm trying to overcome
My truths aren't right and my jeans are too tight
When I pick a fight, I turn to run
All my flawz to see, But You still love, love me.
Even when I sin, I don't fit in
And I've been burned when I've waited my turn
Don't act my age, I don't want to
Call it a phase, call me taboo
Won't do as I'm told to believe
I wear my heart on my sleeve
All my flawz to see, But you still love, Love me.

Your flawz and failures are not the problem. They are proof that you are human and have limitations.

I love the metaphor of the most scarred, dented, tarnished keys, and how much people love them anyway, for the messages they represent. For what they've been through. They carry weight. They carry depth. Keys often get lost, just like we do. And we end up finding them again in the crevices, just as we find ourselves in the divine cracks. They are a reminder of our resilience and magic. We both carry stories of incomparable triumph and victory.

When it comes to failures, imperfections, scars, losses, heartbreak, flaws, inadequacies, and let-downs, I am thankful for them. I will use them as stepping stones of resilience to get back up and push my shoulders back and hold my head high, knowing they are needed and perfect exactly as they are. They are key to my story. They are key to my success. They are key to my discovery. They are key to my breakthrough. They are key to my freedom.

And you are key to yours.

chapter twelve

CAN'T BURN DOWN LOVE

Enjoy the little things, for one day you may look
back and realize they were the big things.
—Robert Brault

As I sit in my front yard on my rusty tree swing, I'm watching bulldozers tear down the house across the street. I'm seven months pregnant, getting bigger by the day, and praying my heavier-than-yesterday self isn't going to send this swing toppling to the ground. (For kicks, fast-forward to a couple months later when I'm still pregnant, and I have now *actually* broken the swing.) I'm ready to welcome my daughter into the world (and hello, ready to be done being pregnant) and thinking about what makes things last. Are there things that really *last* in life?

The woman who lived across the street—a sweet ninety-something mother and grandmother—recently passed away. She raised a family in that home. She outlived three husbands there. She never got divorced, just lived longer. I'm sure she cooked thousands of meals, experienced great joy, and cried thousands of tears

213

in that house. Now she's gone, and I watched as each wall that held her precious memories got smashed to the ground and thrown into a dumpster.

As the house disappeared and the sky became clear where the walls once stood, I couldn't help but think about how her whole world was gone. The only thing that remains is her story and the memories her friends and family hold.

I found myself pondering her life as I pondered my life. There would come a day when I'd be gone from here, and maybe a neighbor would be watching *my* house be torn down. What would I want people to remember about me? What would I want them to think about after I'm gone?

What actually matters to us at the end of our lives? I don't want to look back and wish I was more grateful for all of my blessings: family, work, food, and a home to keep me warm and safe. I don't want to look back and wish I had stressed less about money or my "earth suit" (another way to think of our bodies) or about what others think of me. I don't want to look back and wish I had taken more time to be present. I don't want to look back and wish I had spent more time looking into the eyes of my husband and son and daughter.

I don't want to look back and wish I hadn't wasted precious moments of my life looking at my phone, being negative and critical of myself and others, looking at social media, or comparing myself so much. I don't want to look back and wish I could just let go and surrender and be grateful for the fact that I was given the blessings and body I was given, rather than longing for things that I was never meant to have. I want to actually *do* those things.

Just a few weeks ago, a gardener, who was working in my neighborhood, was showing all his equipment to Brave, who was enthralled. We got to talking, and he was telling me about some of the challenges he's faced. He shared how long and hard he's worked to provide for his family. Covered in dirt and sweat, he motioned toward the homes down the road with their white picket fences and said, "All of this doesn't matter. This is going to fade away. All that matters is love and family."

As simple as that sounds, it touched me that day.

That conversation with the gardener came to mind again as I sat on my swing watching my neighbor's walls literally fade away. It was true what he had said: the material stuff doesn't last. What matters and what lasts are memories, quality time with the people you care about, and love. Love is what lasts. When I think about my neighbor who passed away, I have to believe that her love will live beyond her. Her love will live on through her children, her grand-children, and through a legacy that lasts much longer than a house.

Lately everyone has been talking about Marie Kondo's Netflix show, *Tidying Up with Marie Kondo*, which is based on her book. Funny story: Brave goes to the same preschool as Marie Kondo's daughter, which for *once* makes me feel like a superstar mom since I imagine Marie to be the kind of mom who does all the research and would send her daughter to the best school available. My evil genius plan (now available for the world to see) is to convince Brave and Satzuki to fall in love so I can have Marie Kondo as my in-law and get her help organizing my life forever.

But that's beside the point.

I've only watched the first episode of her show, but the one line that really stood out to me was when she said, "The reason we organize our home is so we can have more time to spend with our families." She said it so calmly and naturally, like everyone already knows that's the goal, but that thought had never occurred to me.

I started thinking about how much time I spend *away* from my family. How much time I spend working and stressing to try to provide for my family, instead of living to actually just spend time with them. Instead of being present and fully alive with them.

One afternoon, I challenged myself to put down my laptop promptly at 5 p.m. so I could go play in the front yard with my husband and son, which I embarrassingly rarely do. We kicked the ball back and forth a few times, found snails on our lemon tree, and smelled the flowers for about an hour. We were bright-eyed, filled with joy, and alive. I felt so at peace that evening. Who knew meeting slugs in my yard could bring more happiness in life than meeting Oprah? (No offense, O—you're still the Queen, and I still want to be your BFF.)

Where is that peace in the other 98 percent of my life?

When I actually let myself spend time in my home, I had a revelation. I had struggled to feel settled in our home. We had downsized in our recent move, and now we were adding a little girl to our family. I also worried about safety since the house is near a busy street where burglaries and car break-ins are known to happen. I let discontent and comparison get the best of me.

But after I put down my laptop in order to play with Colin and Brave, the moment I took time to *be there*, to literally be in my front yard for longer than five minutes, I enjoyed my home. It became a gift.

For the first time in almost two years of living there, I started feeling like maybe my home wasn't so bad. I sat outside again the following week and met a few neighbors who have lived in the neighborhood for over twenty years. One man said he thinks we have the best neighborhood in town.

Since I had been comparing our home to my friends with bigger, better, and safer homes, I had been missing out. Our home was a special place.

Sure, I could still hear and see the freeway, its sideline fence, and the trash at the end of my block. But it didn't matter anymore. All that mattered was the look in Brave's bright eyes and how happy he was that Colin and I were exploring with him. Then, to top it off, suddenly I had a surge of energy to cook dinner for Colin and Brave, which is basically as rare as the apocalypse. So we cooked a meal and ate together.

Maybe that's it. Maybe that's the answer. Clearing away all the work, comparison, drive, and pride. Not living for the "highs" that come with worldly success but making room to really *live*. To enjoy the small, simple, precious moments.

I wrote and recorded a song for an EP once called, "Is This The Good Life?" and at the time I wrote the verses, I was thinking about all the things I wanted to overcome, but then, when I got to the chorus, I began thinking about how so many of us live for thrills or addictions or highs that will never satisfy.

Maybe I will face the dragon
Maybe I will run away
Maybe I will fight the good fight
You put your troubles in your hash pipe
Anything to make it alright.
Screaming in the bathroom
Covered up in perfume
Is this the good life? Is this the good life?
Pour another excuse
Cranberries and Grey Goose
Is this the good life? Is this the good life?

Since I had to have a C-section with Brave, I really wanted to try for a VBAC delivery with Love. My doctor wasn't confident I'd be able to and said she still thought I'd need a C-section. I strategically picked out a FAITH Giving Key to wear during birth, to help fight the fear I was experiencing. I now call it my "keeping key" since I'm never giving it away to anyone. It has my birth sweat on it! I'll probably pass it on to Love one day when she's older. That key, mixed with my athlete-fighter-girl mentality kicked in, and I felt like I was back at the Junior Olympics, about to run the race of a lifetime. I was determined and pushed and pushed so hard, Colin was shocked and impressed. Love came out perfect.

The recovery process provided another opportunity to teach me what true, tested love in a relationship really is. This is not the easy, early stage of immature "love." This is the "I'll clean your diarrhea off the floor" love. This is the real, dirty, ugly, beautiful, vulnerable love. The "I'll hold your hand as your scream and cry and get five catheters in in six days and help you empty your catheter bag into the toilet" love. The "I'll go buy you Depends and hemorrhoid pads" love.

I'm still practicing gratitude with Colin. Sometimes it doesn't come easy. Sometimes it's a choice to have a healthy relationship. This has been a season to show us what true love is. It isn't a fairy-tale infatuation that fades. It isn't always a feeling. With two kids, and after labor and delivery, it's sometimes about cleaning up blood, groceries, poop, catheters, sleepless nights, cooking, cleaning, grocery runs, countless medication and healing aid pick-ups, all while working our butts off to provide for our family. It's imperfect and messy—and yes, we still fight like hell—but I'm grateful. We continue to put in the hard work to fight the good fight for love. Both our love and our daughter, Love.

When it comes to family life, I'm not the poster child (as you've gathered by now), but I'm learning, one day at a time.

One day, my sister-in-law, Kenda, and I took the kids to Chick-fil-A. We sat there chatting, and I asked her how she and her husband, Aaron, have been doing. Her reply has stayed with me.

She said, "We're doing fine. Life isn't always extraordinary. Sometimes it's just day-to-day. But then you wind up being married for twenty-five years, and *that's* extraordinary."

We both sat there for a minute, letting the words settle in. I was thinking about what it would feel and be like to say I'd been married for twenty-five years, to have a love that has lasted that long and all the fruits that come with it. Wouldn't that be extraordinary? Often times good things are not easy.

The day-to-day can be stressful and monotonous—alarm clocks, flossing teeth, bills, and flushing toilets—but then, the next thing you know, you look around and realize you've built something beautiful.

The hard thing about building something beautiful is that, in order to do it, you have to slow down to see clearly. I find it hard to slow down all of the responsibilities I've accumulated through the years, so I'm usually still spinning by the time I get home. When I sit down to play with Brave, it's hard to even get my heart rate to slow down or my thoughts to stop racing long enough to be present, much less enjoy what I'm doing there.

But the other day, while I was on the floor with Brave, it occurred to me that I had a teacher sitting right in front of me. Brave and I were building a castle with LEGOs (and by castle, I mean we were stacking LEGOs on top of each other in a straight line). Watching Brave, I wondered what my life would be like if I approached the world with the same simple wonder and curiosity that he has. What if I could stop and play and think like a child— what if I could be in awe of the simple things? I want to think, "Wow, look at that red color that's so magical in between the green and the blue. And wow, look how tall this is. And wow, we built this. We built this together."

I did not get the gene for being good at "mom crafts." I've decided it must have been distributed to all my other mom friends at the birth of their first child, but it missed me. I once saw a mom on Instagram place her kid's lunch portions on separate doilies with printed messages they'd be surprised with after each bite. That rocked my world. I feel proud of myself for just cutting up grapes so that Brave doesn't choke and remembering to put his name on his lunchbox. But DOILIES? Never would have crossed my mind. I swear, some moms get a special power at birth—like they were given a gene that made them enjoy scrapbooking. Not me.

In an effort to continue to challenge myself into this new season, I decided to ease myself into "playing" by starting an art project for work. I found a can of old house paint, and on some plain printer paper, I painted: "Today is a good day to love."

While I was painting, I gave Brave markers to draw. He drew for a bit but quickly grew frustrated that I was painting my own thing, instead of painting with him. So I quit painting and sat down on the floor to play . . . *drumroll, please* . . . yes, LEGOs again. We then played counting games together and practiced the ABCs. We read books and talked about the names of different animals. He lit up with pride.

I felt such peace and deep joy, like I do during the simple evenings in my front yard, and I realized that maybe one of the reasons I keep myself busy with work is because I'm *afraid* to slow down. Maybe I'm afraid to really notice. Maybe I'm afraid to see the hurt that comes along with simply living—my own pain, friends who are hurting, parents who are hurting, a world that is hurting.

You may remember the Woolsey Fire in the greater Los Angeles area in November 2018. It spread fast because of the winds and dry ground. So fast, in fact, that many people didn't have time to get away. Not only were their homes burned with everything inside, but their lives were in danger as they raced to safety. Their pets and livestock, in many cases, were killed. Tragically, three people lost their lives.

When this was all happening, I started to see friends and acquaintances posting about their homes being burned to the ground. One post was from a swimsuit model, who was also a mother, and whom I followed on Instagram. Earlier that month, I'd been salivating over the interior design of her new, custom-built Malibu home. I felt jealous looking at the photos of her giant closets, custom-made to fit all of her earthly treasures; her gorgeous, custom bathtub to fit her babies; and the high-end, custom furniture that filled her home. I fantasized looking at the pictures and thought to myself, "Wow, she must have *the life*."

But then I saw on Instagram that her house and every single one of those things had burned in the fire. I was snapped out of my daydreaming and reminded that everything we have is disposable. Nothing lasts forever. We can lose everything in an instant, but the one thing that never dies is love. You can't burn down love.

But what does this mean for us, practically speaking? Does it mean we shouldn't have physical possessions? That we don't aspire to them? That we pretend not to want them? That we don't enjoy them? Does it mean that our physical lives and physical bodies and physical possessions don't have an impact on us emotionally and spiritually? Obviously not. I still have a lot to learn, but I'm starting to see that sometimes it's the physical things in our lives (having them or losing them) that force us to look beyond. And it's what's *beyond* that fulfills and heals our souls.

I don't just mean with career purpose, either. Somewhere along this journey I started to get the sense that, when it came to my breast issues, there was still more healing to do. I wanted to find healing for myself, obviously, but I also wanted to find healing for my daughter, who was due any day. For my son. For my husband and this beautiful thing we're building together. For my employees, who are watching me (Lord help them). And for you, who are wondering what it means that you have not yet quite made peace with your body or are seeking healing in an area of your life that feels unresolved.

So I booked a long session with my old therapist, Ann, and told her I was ready to dive deep on my quest to get some serious and lasting healing. On the way there, Colin texted me, saying, "I have been feeling you should do something ceremonially with Ann, a closing this chapter of your life kinda thing. Could be very powerful."

So I walked into Ann's office open to the idea but wondering what kind of ceremony this might be since Ann is also a Christian, and I wasn't aware of any Christian ceremonies for closing certain seasons of life.

The first words out of her mouth when I walked in were, "Your pregnant body is sumptuous."

Yes, I had to google the definition of *sumptuous*. It means splendid, lavish, deluxe, magnificent, gorgeous, grand, extravagant, lush. In other words, it's my new favorite word.

We were off to a great start. I shared Colin's idea with her, and she loved it. She said there are a lot of reasons to have a ceremony.

She told me we are sensate beings (i.e. perceived by the senses). We aren't just one level. We think. We feel. We are tactile. We speak in body language. We are holistic. The act of ceremony covers all of these bases. It doesn't just cover the head. We are a country of thinkers. We stay in the mind most of the time. The cultures in Italy, France, and Mexico are more feelers. A ceremony or ritual connects more of these pieces. If we are just in the mind, we are missing out.

Ann said it was intuitive that Colin sensed there should be a ceremony of some sort. It wasn't just in the mind. He could *feel* it.

The first thing I did was pull out a photo of my deformed boobs and show it to Ann, almost as if to say, "See? How can I possibly heal emotionally, feel love for my body and self, much less ever feel sexy again looking like *this*?"

"It feels hopeless," I told Ann.

"That is the line of demarcation," she said. "The line in the sand. Our culture demands we be flawless and airbrushed. The reality is, breasts are about nurturing. Breasts are close to the heart, and you're all about heart."

When I used to see Ann regularly—ten years prior to this day—she had me make a sand tray. She had hundreds of objects for me to choose from to put on the tray. There was an object for nearly everything life has to offer: food, houses, every type of person and animal, riches, awards, all sorts of flowers, every superhero figurine, and so many more items. I chose to make my sand tray with all hearts. Everything that was a heart or heart-shaped, I put on my tray. Ever since then, Ann's always reminded me that I'm "all heart."

Thinking about it now, it almost seems *impossible* that my main deformed breast on the left side has always been right on top of my heart.

I sat there, stunned, holding my hand over my heart.

Meanwhile, Ann shared a story of a woman who had breast implants for thirty years, then got breast cancer. Based on new and innovative tests, the doctor was convinced it was largely due to having the implants in for so long. Ann turned to me.

"Caitlin, you have to ask yourself, what is most valuable to you? The worst part of this is not your actual breasts. It's how you *feel* about your actual breasts."

"That's true. It's also my narrative about them. It's not only that I *feel* I'm flawed. I *think* I'm flawed beyond healing."

"What you react to is simply a mirror, revealing what you need to work on. So think of that doctor who looked at you after your last surgery and reacted so strongly. It's not a matter of her thinking you're disgusting. Who knows or cares what she thinks? It's a spiritual mirror. It's reflecting back to you what *you* think. So until you clear the mirror, it's your responsibility to say, 'I love my breasts.'"

"It doesn't hurt when Colin says it too," I said, laughing.

"Of course not!"

"And he does. All the time."

"That's because he's a good husband. You can even ask him to say that to you, Caitlin. Ask him to say, *I love your breasts, Caitlin.* Ask him to say it all the time until you finally start to believe it."

I told her I felt like I couldn't do that.

"You teach best what you need to learn."

I sat with that for a minute. Ann was referring to the fact that for so long, I had been waving the Love Your Flawz flag. This was how I had connected with people beyond me; it was my message; it was the thing I believed in the most. But was I really living it out? Was I loving my own flaws?

"How do you love your flaws?" I asked.

"This is a spiritual battleground. To say you are enough just the way you are. You were fated to have breasts like this. Who knows why? Who needs to know?"

We both sat in silence for a few moments.

"It's not just about breasts," Ann continued. "It's about loving yourself, no matter how ugly or insignificant you feel. Being open to the synchronicities that come to you. If you fight the natural course of your destiny, you will just keep spiraling downward. *You can change the course.*"

She was right. I knew she was right. But even though I was there in my mind, I wasn't quite there in my heart just yet. (Pun intended.)

"How can I have a *heart* for my breasts? How can I nurture myself?" I asked.

"What do you think?"

"It feels trite to just look in the mirror and say, 'I love my body,' or 'I love my boobs.' It doesn't feel enough. It doesn't feel like it will work."

"Maybe by completing this book, you're completing something in yourself. Maybe this is part of your path to healing."

That sounded true.

"You want to try Colin's ceremony idea?" she asked.

"Sure!"

Ann took out a small, white tea light candle. She said she was lighting a candle for my left breast. As a symbol of bringing light to it. To help me be open to loving it. She asked me if I felt like I could take that in, and then blow it out when I felt ready to *let it all go.*

I sat with it. I tried to "let it all in" and receive the healing so I could "let it all go." But honestly, I kept getting stuck wondering what a candle had to do with any of it.

Finally I said, "I still feel like I don't understand how this will help me."

"You don't have to understand. That's in the *head.* Every atom, molecule, and neurotransmitter in your body will respond to it because there's a perceptual shift inside you. There is a disatunement in your body that you hate, and perhaps God has given you this flaw to have mastery over it to teach to others."

That struck a chord with me. I felt myself start to soften. I even felt my eyes get a little misty, thinking about who I might be able to help heal because I had done my own healing work.

"You're holding on for dear life and won't surrender. You're holding on like, *Who would Caitlin be without it?*"

"Wow," I said. "You're right. I literally don't know who I'd be without it."

"Everybody's flawed. Everyone has their 'thing' to apply this to. If you truly love this left breast and let yourself believe that you don't have to be perfect to be loved, then you have surrendered, and that's grace. Grace is beyond us. It's synchronicity. Keep your eyes open for it. If you hold on to that flaw, you'll never find the peaceful pool at the end of the line. That will be your fly in the ointment. If you don't let go, it will magnify and get bigger and bigger."

The peaceful pool at the end of the line. I loved those words she spoke over me. I felt myself soften even a little bit more. I needed to surrender it. I was fighting it and holding on to it so tightly that it was scarring my entire *whole-ness* so to speak. I felt like a scarred *person* because of it. Not just a person with a scarred boob. Surrender, accept, release. Surrender, accept, release, I kept telling myself. So I don't pass it down to my daughter.

"My daughter's name is Love," I told Ann. "We haven't told anyone, but I'm telling you. I have to master this. For her."

"Why did you name her Love?"

"Because what is better than love? Absolutely nothing. It is the most precious commodity on the planet. The meaning of life. Without love, there is no meaning and no purpose. "

"Why don't you talk to Love?" Ann suggested.

So I did.

"Love, I have a flaw that I used to hate. It used to disgust me. Though I don't like it and wouldn't choose it, I have chosen and committed to love my whole body and whole self." And I added, "In *spite* of it."

"YES!" Ann yelled.

"Or even *because* of it," I continued, feeling energized by Ann's enthusiasm. "That's what makes me lovable."

"YES! YES! YES!"

"I'm not only surrendering to it, but I'm also choosing to be *grateful* for it. Because that's what has made me unique, one of a kind, truly special, and lovable. It's not a lie I'm forcing myself to say: *I love my body and self.* It's actual *truth.* That I am lovable because it is a holistically beautiful thing. If I look at my deformed breast objectively, by itself, singled out like I always have, I won't see the beauty. But if I look at it holistically, and what it's created in me, what it's produced in me—compassion, empathy, a sense of humor, a deep well to better understand people's pain, and the ability to encourage and love others more deeply—that is a beautiful and complete thing. It is actually a GIFT."

"YES! I HAVE GOOSEBUMPS!" Ann shouted.

I beamed.

"This is called *empowerment*," she said. "You have just empowered yourself. This is graduate work in spirituality that you're taking on."

Maybe I got that MBA, after all.

If it was in that session that I found empowerment, it was over Thanksgiving that I realized what true joy, peace, and contentment felt and meant. Our plan was to go to Johnny and Virginia's, our best friends, who also have a two-year-old who is Brave's best friend.

Johnny made us a home-cooked meal, and we all gathered around their table, just the six of us. We were all in pajamas. We talked and laughed while we ate turkey, then had a dance party in their quaint little living room. It was a night of embracing and enjoying our little families and our most special friendships. Dancing in our onesie pajamas was the most joy I have felt in years and years.

When I reflect back on that night, I'm reminded that everything I've been working so hard for—all the sleepless nights over employees who had left disgruntled and employees who missed target projections, the broken dreams mixed with all the high highs of Starbucks deals and Oprah affirmations and Nordstrom—none of it really mattered. No high could ever compare to this high of my little family and our friends dancing in a little apartment on Thanksgiving. It was simple. It was beautiful. And it was perfect.

One of my favorite quotes from Saint Francis of Assisi is:

> Make me an instrument of Your peace;
> Where there is hatred, let me sow love;
> Where there is injury, pardon;
> Where there is doubt, faith;
> Where there is despair, hope;
> Where there is darkness, light;
> And where there is sadness, joy . . .
> that I may not so much seek
> To be consoled as to console;
> To be understood, as to understand;
> To be loved, as to love.

I am coming to believe, more than ever, that this is the secret to life: to be an instrument of peace, pardon, faith, hope, light, joy, and love (all the words on The Giving Keys). Therein lies freedom.

And so, maybe the new definition of success is just as Saint Francis of Assisi describes, alongside my little Thanksgiving celebration. A tiny, cozy living room and the bare necessities of connection and love. You have some material things, but you know that at any given moment, all of those things could burn to the ground.

The love you give each other is the love that keeps you bonded forever, and the love we have and always will have is the home that can never be burned down. Maybe, when all is said and done, this is our purpose. No matter what else we do or don't accomplish in our lives, if we don't accomplish *this*—loving one another—we will have missed our greatest purpose.

How will you measure your life?

I recently ran into Kenny "Babyface" Edmonds. I hadn't seen him since my early music years. He met my family and saw The Giving Keys around all of our necks, and I told him all about how the movement got started while I was on tour. I told him about the spreading of inspirational words, and how we have now employed over 130 people who are trying to transition out of homelessness.

He kind of chuckled and shook his head and said, "That's *so you.*"

So me. Wow, that really struck a chord.

Thinking back to all the dozens of songs we wrote together, and him hearing my heart about the messages I wanted to share almost twenty years ago, it's amazing that those same messages from the depths of my soul have still come into the world, just in a different package.

I always wanted to write an "official" The Giving Keys song, so I sat down with some of my favorite Nashville writers Fred Wilhelm and Matthew Perryman Jones for a few sessions, shared the evolution of The Giving Keys with them, read through our website's Pay It Forward Stories section, and this song came out:

Pass It On

I've been reading through your stories
Of broken locks and doors we never
thought would open up again
I've been scrolling through the pages
And picturing your faces
We are on our way to being strong
Pass it on
Pass it on

There's a baby barely breathing
And all a mother needs is a reason
to get through another day
Someone's fighting to stay sober
When a stranger out of nowhere gives him
a little hope when his was gone
Pass it on

On and on and on and on and on (x2)

So I'm keeping my eyes open
To every word unspoken
Memories I just can't see beyond
No matter how you're hurt now
Every fire burns out
Even in the darkness there's a dawn
Pass it on

On and on and on and on and on (x2)

I've been reading through your stories
Of failures and glories
You find you had it in you all along . . .

What is the thing that is *so you*? What would it look like for you to run into someone from your past and have them say what Babyface said to me: That's *so you*?

We aren't promised tomorrow. We can't afford to wait until we "feel" qualified (hint: you never really will). So what will you do today? What lights you up and brings light to others?

Take the good, the bad, and the ugly, and wrap it up into your own perfectly flawed masterpiece of a purpose to contribute to the world. Take all your ugly, imperfect insecurities—your so-called Flawz—along with your triumphs, your gifts, your mess-ups, your regrets, your quirks, your stories, along with your thinking you're not educated enough, smart enough, or good enough, and make this your legacy.

Forget thinking you're not the right size to fit into a box. Thank God you don't fit into a box. There will never be another you. There will never be another story like yours.

Your re-purposed, scratched-up, flawed stories can "unlock" your true purpose. Because if you look past your imperfections, you will find your resilience, and that is true beauty. And the world needs more of *that* kind of beauty.

At The Giving Keys offices, we have keys of all kinds in our production area. They are shiny or dappled, sharp or smooth, vintage or modern. But each of them has a unique teeth design that was made to open one door no other key can.

I believe it's the same for us. All of our gifts look different. Each of us were made for unlocking and unleashing something meaningful into the world. Who knew such a small thing could be so powerful?

As I sit here today, having given birth to my new baby girl just a few weeks ago—Love—and I read her *The Giving Tree*, I look forward to instilling in her all the beauty and wonder in her imperfect perfectness, the joy of being present, the beauty in giving—just like my mom did with me, and just like I do with Brave—all snuggled up on the couch as we turn the page, wondering what will happen next, and looking for new, unseen, wondrous ways to pay it forward.